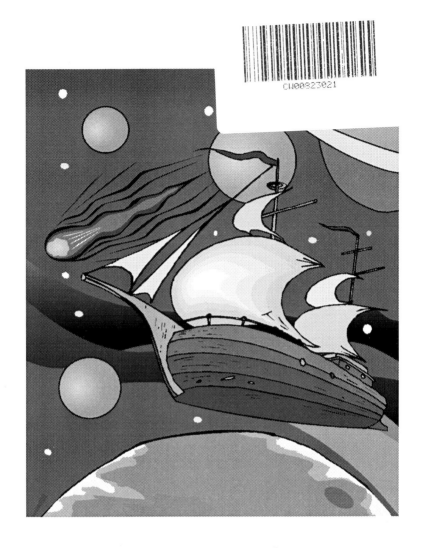

2001: A POETRY ODYSSEY BIRMINGHAM VOL I

Edited by Helen Chatwin

First published in Great Britain in 2001 by
YOUNG WRITERS
Remus House,
Coltsfoot Drive,
Peterborough, PE2 9JX
Telephone (01733) 890066

HB ISBN 0 75433 052 4
SB ISBN 0 75433 053 2

FOREWORD

Young Writers was established in 1991 with the aim to promote creative writing in children, to make reading and writing poetry fun.

This year the 2001: A Poetry Odyssey competition again proved to be a tremendous success with over 50,000 entries received nationwide.

The amount of hard work and effort put into each entry impressed us all, and is reflective of the teaching skills in schools today.

The task of selecting poems for publication was a difficult one but nevertheless, an enjoyable experience. We hope you are as pleased with the final selection in *2001: A Poetry Odyssey Birmingham Vol I* as we are.

CONTENTS

Christopher Smith	42
Anthony McVay	42
Jay Yeomans	43
Rachael Pinson	43
Kieran Hannon	44
Jamie Nolan	45
Paul Dillon	46
Simon Brooke	46
Jade Carr	47
Denise Ward	48
Matthew Hardwick	49
James Hopkins	50
Sean Mulcahy	50
Laura Kilroy	51
Katie Lindsay	52
Stuart Bartlett	52
Rebecca Eschoe	53
Helen Armstrong	54
Reaha McLarty	55
Joseph Murray	56
Peter Murtagh	57
Chelsea Gaffey	58
Ben Tranter	59
Richard Cox	60
Andrew Bailey	61
Daniel Tolster	62
Terence Ryan	63
Elouise Teeling	63
Shane Austin	64

Bishop Challoner RC School

Aarron Wynne	64
Ryan Wilson	65
Clara McDonald	65
Elisha Rogers	66
Joe Baker	66

Sophie Yardley	114
James Parker	114
Anthony Poole	115
Jason Coley	115
Ian Barrett	116
Jodie Killeen	116
Chris Lawrence	117
Charlotte Baker	117
Aaron Ellis	118

Great Barr School

Joanne Paintin	119
David Bonner	119
Samantha Dangerfield	120
Laura Denton	120
Stephanie Somerfield	121
Harry Walker	122
Keisha Lawrence	122
Lisa Speak	123
Paul Eames	124
Amy Poyner	125
Sharanjit Sahota	126
Dionne Chisholm	126
Shareen Lawrence	127
Dee Gallagher	128
Nateesha Toora	128
Emily Wilkes	129
Amandeep Sander	130
Joanne Beddows	130
Julie Parry	131
David Ellson	132
Justina Maynard	133
Daniel Ullah	134
Terri Gray	134
Craig Wiggins	135
Jonathan Greene	136

The Poems

LIFE

Life is a living thing,
If you think you have not got
A life you are wrong.

Life is a generation
It is a form of nature,
And nature is a form of life.

When you are born you are
Starting a life, a life that you
Want to go on and on.

Life is a living thing,
So use it.

When you get to see the light of
When you were born,
Life is a living thing,
So use it and don't lose it.

James McNutt (15)

MISUNDERSTOOD

I am misunderstood with pain in my life,
I am misunderstood, who cares?
I look at the world with pain in my eyes,
I am misunderstood, who cares?

Not I.

Luke Gwinnett (16)

BLIND MAN AND HIS DEAF FRIEND

Look out says the blind man to his deaf friend
The blind man says he can't hear me, he ain't wearing his glasses
His deaf friend runs with his glasses
And his deaf friend walks with his hearing aid
Then the deaf friend drops on the floor
The blind man helps his deaf friend up
The deaf friend thanked his friend and put on his glasses
The blind man said 'You're welcome' and put his hearing aid on
Then a lady walks by with a dog and
The blind man said 'What a lovely dog.'
The lady said 'Thank you.'
The blind man said 'You've got nice legs, for a pool table.'
Then she said, 'I didn't know you can see with your eyes closed.'
The blind man said 'Yeah you know it ya fool.'

Then the woman realised that the man was blind and noticed
He had a friend and said hello, no answer and she said it again
Still no reply so she then realised that they were deaf and blind
Then she noticed the blind man had a hearing aid
And the deaf friend was wearing glasses.
So she suggested that they change over.
She walked over and took the blind man's glasses off his deaf friend
And took deaf friend's hearing aid off the blind man and in the end
Both could see and hear again.

Shantelle Reece (16)

REASON WHY

Reason,
Why?
Just because I love you,
That's de reason why
Ma soul is full of colour
Like de wings on a butterfly.

Just because I love,
That's de reason why
Ma heart's a fluttering aspen
Leaf
When you pass by.

Joleen Mahon (12)

THIS FEELING!

Is this a feeling
Which is always there,
It's so hard to say
If you don't really care.

I try so hard to do my best,
And rise above all the rest.
This is a feeling which may never die,
And will always stay to make you cry.

It will eat you away,
Till this very day,
And scar your arm,
And the rim of your palm.

This feeling is there,
Almost everywhere
You can't run nor hide,
It will eat at your pride.

You try to find help
In so many ways,
But people do not hear,
Just comment on your
Emotional displays.

Kerry Marklew (16)

DO THE CRIME, DO THE TIME

I did a robbery Christmas Day
I got locked up and Queen Road I stayed
They told me that crime doesn't pay
They tried to show me the right way
For the things I did on my negative day
They took me to Kingsmere for two days
But for four months I stayed and prayed
Watching people come and go night and day
I feel depressed so I say
Crime doesn't pay
You know what they say
Do the crime,
Do the time
I remain at Kingsmere to this very day
For the silly thing I did on my negative day
I hope that someone will show me the right way
Because I did not enjoy my negative day.

Crushi Badley (16)

I WAS HERE

I was here but now I'm not
I'm round the corner smoking pot
I've left this rhyme to make a point
Life is s**t without a joint.

I was here but now I've gone
I've left my name to turn you on.

I was here but now I've gone
I am just a lyrical don.

Warren Burnside (12)

PRISON

I feel sad
I hate being locked up because I miss friends and family
But I won't be here forever
When I get out I will have a fag,
When I get out I will see my family,
When I get out I will go to McDonald's,
When I get out I will be glad,
When I get out I will be happy,
When I get out I will be free,
When I get out I will be on my house phone,
When I get out I will be out all day and night,
When I get out I will be like a bird,
When I get out I will be having fun.
Now I don't feel so sad.

Sophie McCone (14)

MY SCHOOL POEM

I am going to secondary school
And I have to know all the rules.
I think it's going to be very cool
My school's got a swimming pool.
I've had my ups and downs in that primary school
I'll remember the pencil, the silly tool,
My friend's such a fool,
In that school.
I'll remember the mule at safari zoo
That said moo!
I'd like to thank Mr McNally
And the teachers too
Goodbye St. Bernadette's, I shall miss you!

Asim Maqsood (11)

A World For The Future

Everything grew a million years ago
Nothing has grown since
We have no need for life
But we have metal
All wrapped up in chains
In a million years time
All will be replaced
Like the bike got replaced by the car
Humans by robots
Plants by fire
The sun will be a cube of electricity
Blinding, deafening with its electronic buzz
Water will be rushing from bottom to top
We will see potatoes falling from the clouds of toxic gas
Choking anything that dares to grow
There will be no need for schools
We will be born with the information we need
We won't be born
We will be made from pieces of rust lying in the black sky
Humans will disappear as quick
As dreams go from the puzzle that we call our mind
Feelings and emotions will be swallowed
By the hole of pain and suffering the world will turn into
Everything grew a million years ago
Nothing has grown since
This is our home
We are the rats
The world is our sewer full to the brim of sewage.

Tanya Stezhka (12)

FRIENDS

My friends are a gift from above,
And I'll keep that within my heart,
I will always treasure their love,
Nothing will ever tear us apart.

Friends like these are so hard to find,
Which is why I feel blessed inside,
They will endlessly be on my mind,
And this I promise I will never hide.

Even when we go our separate ways,
They are going to remain with me forever,
I will cherish all the special days,
We had when we were together.

Although I don't want to let my friends go,
The time has come to say goodbye,
But I just want you all to know,
My feelings for you will never die.

All my friends mean the world to me,
And in my eyes that's really something,
This poem is to make them see,
How much joy and happiness they bring.

Rebecca Thompson (15)

FOUR WAYS OF LOOKING AT A TREE

A withered, old man, reaching out for help.
A giant, waving to his companions.
A farmer sowing his seeds in the field.
A man with an afro-hairdo, rippling in the breeze.

Ian Clarke (12)
Archbishop Ilsley RC School

HARRY POTTER'S SCHOOL

H ogwarts is a great school with wizards and witches that learn magic
at school.

O ut of all the schools Hogwarts is the best

G reat transport to get there, a train that takes you through a magic
land

W ith secret passages all over the place you can't be late for lessons.

A fter the first year Harry didn't want to go home because it was so
good

R on, Harry's best friend as well never wants to go home

T ransfiguration is the best lesson for Harry

S ettling in isn't hard when you're at Hogwarts.

Glenn Jones (11)
Archbishop Ilsley RC School

MY POEM ABOUT LOVE

Love is a rose as sweet as can be
If you can touch it you can be free.

Looking at your life trying to see
Is love God's blessing or is it a mystery?

Love is with family or even with your friends
But if you are close love will never end.

Broken hearts they might just mend
But if it don't it will drive you up the bend.

So if you are touched make the most of your luck
Because there's mostly happiness in love.

Alana Hanley (12)
Archbishop Ilsley RC School

THE THING

I saw my dad frown
We were going to the seaside
With the sand and the tide
But what shall we do now we all had to decide,
So we got out a board game Runaway Bride
But at that moment we all nearly died,
There were no pieces in Runaway Bride
And at that moment we all started to blubber.

'Fear not!' said Dad 'I'll go and get another!'

Dad reached for his wallet and went for the door,
But then he saw something lying on the floor.
He went and told Mom.
But where had it come from?
Dad picked it up and put it in a cage
You could see on its face that it was full of rage.

We thought it was a large spider
But as we came nearer, its mouth opened wider
We thought it was hungry and gave it some food,
Maybe that would cheer up the sad little dude.
But at that moment it spat out some plastic,
Not to mention some wood and elastic!
We decided to keep it and use it as a bin
We gave it its dinner, some wood and a tin.

Next morning we came down to see it
It had gone! Then so be it!
It was a sad little creature,
It made such a wonderful feature!
Will I ever see it again? Who knows?
Well, that's the way life goes!

Todd Geary (11)
Archbishop Ilsley RC School

THE STORM

It was hot and humid late one night
He couldn't get to sleep.
The air was still, the sky was dark
His bed clothes were in a heap
He heard a rumble in the sky,
The room lit up with lightning
He didn't like the sound of it
It was very frightening.
All at once the rain came down
It sounded very loud,
It hit the windows in my room
It must have been that cloud
The air cooled down
The storm passed
Time to go to sleep, at last.

Laura Flynn (13)
Archbishop Ilsley RC School

THE GARDEN

I am walking past the garden,
My spine begins to jump,
The gate is screaming in the wind,
The leaves are waving an evil wave,
The shutters fighting against the windows,
And the wind whispers in my ear
The garden.

Stuart Clover (11)
Archbishop Ilsley RC School

FOOTBALL

Saturday what a day,
It's time for footy hip, hip, hooray,
Are we at home or are we away?
I don't care 'cause we'll cheer anyway,
Come on you blues,
Put on your shoes,
And please, please
Don't let us lose.
When it comes half-time
We'll sing our rhyme,
And then it's back out,
And we'll give you a shout,
Blue and white,
It's been quite a night,
Hip, hip, hooray,
You've done it alright.

David Taylor (12)
Archbishop Ilsley RC School

OUR WORLD

Our world is an unending place with wonders all around,
Listen close and you might hear Mother Nature's sound.
If you seek you may not find her but you'll always know she's there,
Drifting, drifting through the trees, the wind blowing through her hair.
Though we have left you grieving over your destroyed power,
Please do not desert us in the lonely hour.
We have done you plenty wrong, through you have done us none,
You will remain forever trying to unite the world as one.

Carrie Ingram-Gettins (11)
Archbishop Ilsley RC School

WAR

God put us on Earth as sister and brother,
So why do we go on killing each other?

Why can't countries just get along
Without using bullets or bombs?

All the soldiers getting hurt and needing help,
When will it hit them they're only killing themselves.

It only takes a few men, to not be friends
And not shake hands and
Everything results in planes and tanks.

Everyone being killed, all the people
More and more, this is it, this is war.

John Egan (13)
Archbishop Ilsley RC School

THE EMPTY BATTLEFIELD

The field is now empty calm and still.
The sky is mournful and grey.
The bodies are lifeless, their determination gone,
But the cries of their last moments still fill the air.
The guns covered in blood as red as wine
They shoot their last bullets for the brave and yet scared.
The battles carries on their souls not at rest
They won their living battle
But the battle for a place in Heaven still carries on.

Ellie Marklow (11)
Archbishop Ilsley RC School

AUTUMN

Autumn leaves are falling
From the trees so high,
Deep brown and golden
Falling from the sky.
Gracefully they fall,
Twirling round and round.

And when you tread on them
They crunch into the ground.
After trees are bare
Berries acorns, grow.

But soon the leaves will come again
And grow, grow, grow.

Christopher Jefferies (13)
Archbishop Ilsley RC School

EIGHT WAYS OF LOOKING AT A TORCH

A lamp that guides the cars along the road.
A ceiling light that lights up the room for people.
A sun to light up the whole world for God to see his people.
A rainbow that leaps over a waterfall.
A crystal that reflects the beams of the sun.
A tree trunk that stands up through all conditions.
A ten pin bowling that fades away when the ball hits.
A snooker cue that gets pushed around.

Daniel Tully (12)
Archbishop Ilsley RC School

My Soaps And Sitcoms!

Eastenders the soap on BBC 1
If it wasn't for the Slaters it would now be long gone.

Friends is a sitcom set in the States
They all live together as very good mates.

Homer Simpson is thought to be funny
But some people think he's kind of a dummy.

Brookside the soap is set in the north-west
Some soaps fans think this is the best.

Emerdale shows Yorkshire trouble and strife
With the Woolpack pub centre of village life.

Granada TV transmits Coronation Street
The Rovers Return is where the locals meet.

Friends and The Simpsons I think are the best
They're miles better than all the rest.

Danielle Reid (12)
Archbishop Ilsley RC School

A Few Ways Of Looking At A Bullet Train

The bullet train is as fast as the speed of light.
Its nose is as pointy as a bird's beak.
Its like a speed boat gliding through the water.
It scares the passengers and it is as scary as a fair ride,
As it bombs through the railway line flying down the track.

Paul Whitehead (12)
Archbishop Ilsley RC School

FOOTBALL

He's running down the wing
All the crowd are singing
He's got halfway so far
He feels like a pile of tar
He's got past his first player
He was not much of a match
There are three more players ahead
He does not really care
But if he gets past them
He will be man of the match
He dribbles all three players
He's running faster and faster
He gets to the goalkeeper
And shoots
It's, it's, it's
It's a goal!

Thomas Flaherty (13)
Archbishop Ilsley RC School

TEN WAYS OF LOOKING AT A TELE

A box, that you put things in.
A paper where you get information from.
It's where you see exciting things
A comedian, that's the entertainment.
A school because you learn things
Reality, shows are like it.
A cinema, movies and lots of people watching.
A computer, interactive and digital.
A book, different storylines.
Birmingham City, it's wicked!

Ashleigh Colgan (12)
Archbishop Ilsley RC School

ROCKY RULES WRESTLING

R ock
O n the
C lock
K icking
Y our

R oody poo candy coated beep!
U nder
L ights
E very night
S o run.

W restling
R ules
E verything
S ometimes not
T azz
L ooks like he
I s a mad
N utter
G roaning.

Daniel Rhodes (12)
Archbishop Ilsley RC School

PARENTS VS KIDS

Parents are a pest,
We never get a rest
They think they're just the best
Better than all the rest
'Eat your greens' they shout
'If you don't you'll get a clout'.
Then you'll know about it kids

Kids make a fuss
They think they're better than us
They're on the computer all day
All they want to do is play
'Tidy that Lego away
Now!'

Jason Scattergood (12)
Archbishop Ilsley RC School

WHY CAN'T I?

Why can't I do all my work right?
It's not that big goal it's in my sight.

Why can't I do my homework every day?
I try and I try
But when I hand it in there's no reply.

Why can't I have brilliant writing?
I've got to practice it isn't a matter of liking.

Why can't I love my work?
When I look at it I just smirk.

Why can't I listen to the Sir or Miss?
Except I listen to the latest gossip about a stupid kiss.

Why can't I put my hand up every time?
I think to myself I know that one it's mine.

Why can't I do loads of typing?
I'm too busy messing around, fighting.

It's a simple question
Why?

Richard Whitehouse (12)
Archbishop Ilsley RC School

THE RAIN

The rain drips and drips
It's cold and miserable
I can't go outside because it's wet
Oh where is the sun?
Come out of the cloudy sky
Come down from the heavens
Shine upon us
Evaporate the rain
And give off your heat
But you don't
The rain, the rain it drips and drips
It's cold and foggy and wet
Oh what is this?
The sun out from the heavens
The rain, the rain it disappears
Evaporates
It's warm, it's warm let's rejoice
Oh the powers of the sun.

Mark Hobbins (12)
Archbishop Ilsley RC School

A FEW WAYS OF LOOKING AT A FLOWER

A bright rainbow, brightening the sky
A fruity sweet with a blossom smell
A multicoloured dress smooth and light
A sweet young lady flowing in white
Pink and white mallows ready to eat
A windmill spinning in the wind.

Fiona Hubbard (12)
Archbishop Ilsley RC School

PARENTS

My mom and dad
Always think they know best
Even in the winter
They make me wear a vest.
They're always going on and on
They never give me a break
When I ask for a treat
They won't let me have cake
They say that sweet stuff
Rots your gums
They say you must do as you are told
And send you to bed if you are bold
They look after you in an annoying way
But they never expect any pay
And what sort of world would it be
Without my parents to watch over me.

Liam Green (12)
Archbishop Ilsley RC School

AUTUMN IS COMING

As I wake up in the morning
And I hear the birds singing
And I hear the rustling of the wind.
As I see autumn coming
And the leaves falling off the trees
As they rustle down the street
As the wind blows them all around.

Lee Checkett
Archbishop Ilsley RC School

THE DUSTMAN

My dustman comes on a Wednesday
He take the bins away
He collects the muck
Puts it in his truck
And drives the truck away.

My dustman makes a lot of noise
He's not very discreet
He drives round the street
Once a week
Picking up bags of rubbish.

But there's one dustman
Who does it only when he can
Because he lives in Milan
To try and catch up
On his tan
Because he's the dustbin man.

Paul Herron (13)
Archbishop Ilsley RC School

ALIENS

A is for aim to aim at the enemy
L is for lights to light their spaceship
I   is for ignition to take off into space
E is for exterminator killing our world.
N is for numbers millions of aliens
S is for slime that comes out of their nose.

David Drydale (11)
Archbishop Ilsley RC School

The Winter

The winter has just begun,
There are no more games or fun,
There are leaves on the ground,
Clouds all around,
The rain has replaced the sun.

The day will soon become night,
And the stars they shine so bright,
It's cold outside,
We slip and slide,
The world is a covering of white.

I tuck myself up in bed,
And when I lay down my head,
I dream of the snow,
And places I'll go,
And a fat friendly man dressed in red.

Rebecca Purnell (12)
Archbishop Ilsley RC School

Creation

C   reation began with the Earth
R   eally soon after God made the
E   arth into trees, flowers and animals and even day and night
A   nd then he decided to make man
T   hen woman
I   nto a garden they were placed
O   n every day something new was made
N   ever to be wiped away.

Samantha Oakley (12)
Archbishop Ilsley RC School

COLOURS OF THE RAINBOW

My favourite colour is red,
Nice and warm like my bed,
Next comes yellow like the sun,
It makes me smile even when I'm dull.

Blue reminds me of the sea,
And feeding seagulls on the sand,
Orange is quite nice I think,
That's why it's put in lots of drinks.

Green is the colour of the grass,
Where I play football and catch,
Violet is quite a nice colour,
But when I'm mad it gets duller.

Indigo is like the sky at night
When the stars are shining bright,
These are the colours of the rainbow,
That you can never reach,
But it only appears when there is rain and sun.

Lorenzo Fiorletta (12)
Archbishop Ilsley RC School

THE LITTLE MOUSE

The little mouse
Climbed the candlestick
To eat the tallow
Around the wick.

But when he got up,
He could not get down;
He called his grandmother,
But she was gone.

Then he turned himself
Into a ball,
His little sharp nose
And tail and all.

And rolled right down
Without any fuss,
And went some place else,
That little mouse!

Joel Kempson (12)
Archbishop Ilsley RC School

THE BOY CALLED MITCH

There was a boy called Mitch,
Whose nickname was Titch,
Everyone took the mick,
When he fell in a ditch.

Everyone laughed and called him names,
Especially the big boys who made his nickname,
Why do they do it? Someone asked me,
I said I suppose it is for fun or to embarrass him.

While they took the mick,
I gave him a little tip,
Next time if they take the mick,
Give them a little kick.

Mitch is my brother,
He gave them a kick,
Then they stopped calling him Titch,
And they then called him Mitch,
I shouted hooray!
They have his name right for once.

Colleen Nolan (12)
Archbishop Ilsley RC School

MY FOOTBALL TEAM

My football team are the worst you can get,
We're one-nil down before you can say anything,
Even if we have kick-off.

Our manager is barmy
He hops around like a kangaroo
Our tactics are kangaroo style.

Our football kit! What we don't have a football kit,
Some of us wear blue, some black
So we don't know who's on our team.

The big match for us to play
The match was rigged but we didn't care
If we score we'll go loopy.

It's kick-off time
And we're playing Francis Town
But what there's no one to play
Nooooo!
It's announced a draw.

Phillip Payton (11)
Archbishop Ilsley RC School

QUESTIONS

Why do people die?
And where do people go?
How long do they stay for?
Why doesn't anybody know?

Why do we all live on Earth?
Why not Mars or the moon?
Who decided to live on Earth?
How come no one knows?

Why does it rain?
How come it snows?
Why is there different seasons?
I really want to know.

I have so many questions
But not enough time.
Why do we have questions?
I really had to ask.

Rachel Lingwood (12)
Archbishop Ilsley RC School

NEW CHANGES

Seeing them all older than me,
Makes me wary,
It's hard making new friends
I'll make some soon.

Ball getting kicked around,
Us running away from it,
I get blasted
Oh no the shame.

Lining up waiting for lunch,
Then they all come running out,
Like a herd of elephants.

At last it's home time
The end of a hard,
But interesting day
Meeting a load of new friends.

A poem about how a
New year seven feels about
Their first day!

Kelly Hawkins (12)
Archbishop Ilsley RC School

CREATION

Creation happened long ago
Read the bible and you'll know
God made things that they should grow.
Everything makes up our world
Al things big and small and curled.
We should thank God for
Animals, stars,
The moon and sun.
Friends and families,
Teachers and doctors.
Nature and all of our earth.
Thank you God

Melissa Tumulty (12)
Archbishop Ilsley RC School

MOMS

Don't you just hate moms
All they do is nag and moan at you,
Sometimes I think it's for their own enjoyment
Haven't you noticed they're never happy no matter what
You do or how much effort you put into something?
In their eyes it's always wrong.
Don't you just hate moms,
Even when they're pleased with you all they say is there's
Still room for improvement.
Moms can't live with 'em, can't live without 'em!

Becky Hogan (12)
Archbishop Ilsley RC School

WINTER

The winter was cold,
Snow as cold as ice
Soft snow. Cold wind
Blowing on my face.
I picked up some snow,
Slowly melting in my hand.
My hand went numb.

Cold wind as it
Was blowing snow
Through my hair,
Kids running wild,
Kids throwing snowballs
I watched their feet
Printing footprints in the snow.

I shivered
Watching people
Making snowmen.
And then kicking them
Down again, I saw
Kids on sledges sliding
Down hills, then I saw
It coming at me at
Full speed, it hit me
Like a thousand needles
Going into my face
The winter was very cold.

Ian Lynock (13)
Archbishop Ilsley RC School

FAMOUS

Being famous, should be contagious,
It must be great hearing, the crowd roar,
(By people of all ages)
Getting paid must be a good one,
I mean come on, not
Everything is as fun.
You might dance, scream, run,
And shout and your luck is never out.
You might dribble and tackle
And fall and slide and
Even then you win the battle
But I don't think it's right
The way they all fight.
They make football look silly
And it gives me a fright.

But most of all I'd like to
Be famous, because it's
Contagious!

Christine Perkins (11)
Archbishop Ilsley RC School

JOURNEY'S END

Sitting alone in my chair,
There is no one to care,
The tears I have cried,
To live alone I have tried.

You were always by my side,
The love we felt, we could not hide,
But now you have gone away,
No longer, here, will I stay.

The tablets now a drink
I long not to think,
Of the life I leave behind,
To death I am resigned.

Now, as I fall to sleep,
My memories do I keep,
Of the life I once had,
For I am no longer sad.

Karly Savage (13)
Archbishop Ilsley RC School

THE VERY RUDE BOY

I know a boy, he's just a kid,
But what in the world do you think he did?
The goop he licked his fingers,
The goop he licked his knife,
The goop he talked while eating
He lived an untidy life!
His manners at the table
Were very sad to see
You'd scarce believe a child could act
In such a way as he.

His mom she yelled
His dad he screamed
Excuse your manners his grandfather beamed.
The boy replied I am sick of scoldings
And sendings to bed
Now the grown-ups shall be punished
Instead!

Amy Finn (12)
Archbishop Ilsley RC School

STUNNING THIEF

Your skin is so smooth
It makes me cry
So wonderfully
Wonderfully,
Wonderfully pretty.
Why did you do it to me?
Am I not what I'm meant to be?
I used to have pride and courage
But since you did it to me
My life has been hid by a shadow.
God! Make this all go away
I just want something, something I used to have
I can't shake the memories from my head.
Sometimes I feel, I might be better off dead
I shared my purity
My purity you stole
My purity you gave to *him*!

Ron Rushton (14)
Archbishop Ilsley RC School

NATURE

Nature is from raging rapids
To wonderful waterfalls, little streams
To big open ponds.
To the clouds in the sky
To animals on the ground
Such as tigers and leopards but in
The streams there are colourful fishes
To salmon and herring but in the sea
There are river fish like anglens and gulper eels too
But deeper than that lives whales and great white sharks
To sperm whales to humpback whales as well
Including flounder fish to leopard seals to squids as well.

But in the trees there waits
A jaguar sits in the tree to pounce
On a deer he is so silent he is
Like the rain so he can't be smelt
As he is about to pounce the deer
Runs away so the jaguar runs after it
Eventually he catches it
But life was short for that and the happens the sharks chase little fish
And attack dolphins as well.

Sean Fennell (12)
Archbishop Ilsley RC School

NO, IT'S NOT MY BROTHER!

Mom's in a fuss
Dad won't even speak.
My whole family's still in disbelief.

It's crying again
Oh God! What does it want?
A bottle, a nappy or just some fuss
Whatever it is, I've had enough.

'Oh isn't he cute,' they stop me and say
They think he's my brother
How I wish he was.

My friends call me names, too harsh to repeat,
So many regrets, so many whys?
A simple mistake now my life is ruined
I'd do anything to turn back the time
My teenage years are over and I'm only thirteen.

Sinead Nicholls (15)
Archbishop Ilsley RC School

JIM

There was a boy called Jim who was thrown in the bin,
Hit on the head and felt as if he was dead.
Jim got bullied every day and was thrown in the piles of hay.

On the way home he took out a comb.
They broke it and bend it and threw it away
And called him names all the next day.

He was bullied for days, weeks, months and years
And spend all his time in tears.
He cried for hours on end
And felt like he was going round the bend.

Jim got tired of being picked on and went to his head of year.
He told him not to shed a tear.

At last Jim's troubles came to an end
He would go to school get on
And not go round the bend.

On the way home he could take out his comb and it wouldn't get broke
Or bent and they wouldn't throw it away
And certainly wouldn't call him names all the next day.

Chris Earlis (12)
Archbishop Ilsley RC School

THE ARCTIC

A white duvet is all to be seen,
So still and silent and ever so clean,
A trail of footprints leads to the sea
Where a hungry polar bear is fishing for her tea.

The sun goes down the moon comes out
Peace surrounds all about
Soon life awakes and noise is heard
By the white feathered night bird.
A wolf howls to the crescent moon
He knows silence will overcome soon.

Kelly Jackson (11)
Archbishop Ilsley RC School

GOD'S WORLD

The sky so blue, clouds so white, the sun so high
The sun so bright, the moon, the stars, the planet Mars,
Who made all of this?
God.
The grass, the trees the buzzing bees,
Who made all of these?
God.
The dogs, the cats those horrible rats,
Who made all of these?
God.
The sea, the sand all parts of the land,
Who made all of these?
God.
The people who are homeless and those who are so sad,
Who makes them all so happy?
God.
Who do we think of all the day,
To whom do we kneel down to pray,
Who looks after us while we sleep,
To whom we ask our souls to keep?
God.

Jonathan Walker (11)
Archbishop Ilsley RC School

DIANA

Diana, Diana,
Everyone loved her,
Her sons, boyfriend and family.

She died tragically,
In a car accident,
The bodyguard the only witness.

The world loved her,
She helped the rich and poor,
The sick and ill.

She was once married,
Now she is not,
Charles still loves her.

She helped recover land-mines,
People who lost parts of the body,
Those which were disabled.

Diana, Diana,
Everyone loved her,
Everyone was sad when she

Died.

Mark Jordan (12)
Archbishop Ilsley RC School

AN ALIEN VALENTINE

Dear lover Alien, I love you with your thirteen legs
And your hair so blue and
Your space chocs covered with goo.

In all of inner and outer space
There cannot be such a beautiful gooey face,
With ears stuck on all over the place.

So let me be your satellite
Revolving round you every night,
Tell me yes, oh, tell me soon
For you my dear I'm over the moon.

Liam Bleakman (12)
Archbishop Ilsley RC School

DAYS OF THE WEEK

Oh how sweet it is,
Monday,
Tuesday,
Wednesday,
Thursday,
Friday,
Saturday,
Sunday,
Monday is the slowest day,
Tuesday is not so bad,
Wednesday is a good day,
Thursday is fab,
Friday is supertastic,
Saturday is excellent,
Lots of parties
Party,
Party all day,
All night,
Groovy,
Funky,
Dancing all day,
Time for bed,
Goodnight
I'm gone.

Kelly Connolly (12)
Archbishop Ilsley RC School

MY CHRISTMAS POEM

Emma was excited as Christmas was coming,
The birds above started humming,
There was a chill outside as snow was falling.

The paths are more slippery than before
Oh can't Santa now come through that door,
He can leave the reindeers on the floor.

Twelve hours left there is no one around,
Only my mom's wrapping making a sound,
I got four different presents for my family
And I only spent ten pounds.

I hope I get a Nike coat,
Or even them slippers in a shape of a goat.
I hope I get a lot of money
And a Christmas card that's really funny.

Oh Dad, stop moaning or I'll lock you in the rabbit's cage
Oh yes, please act your age.
Goodnight Mom I did say,
I hope tomorrow I have a good day.

Siobhan O'Keefe (11)
Archbishop Ilsley RC School

BULLYING

Are they here,
Or are they there?
Why is it me?
It's not fair.

Some kick,
Some punch,
But mainly it's names
They must think it's a game.

How do they live with themselves?
I would feel shame,
But for me,
It's the end of the game.

Ian Jackson (13)
Archbishop Ilsley RC School

MY POEM

As I walked towards the plane,
I got closer and closer,
The more I went the faster my heart pounded,
I started to get very scared and afraid,
There it was the door of the plane,
As I reached out I touched the plane door,
I waited for a minute or two,
Then I got on the plane,
My heart was pounding and pounding,
I slowly walked up the plane.
There it was my seat,
I slowly began to sit down,
One minute to take off,
I sat there with fear,
The sweat dripped down my face,
I grabbed on to my seat so hard and tight,
Then the plane started to drive down the runway,
I just froze I couldn't move an inch,
Then the plane started to pick up some speed.

Then all of a sudden the plane took off
At first I closed my eyes,
But once we were in the air I was fine.

Terence Taroni (13)
Archbishop Ilsley RC School

ICE HELL

He and his gang got their skates
Then went to the rink to exchange mates.

The test of performance came
This was his moment of fame.

The seats arose to cheer
As the boy stood in fear.

He stumbled towards the start
Oh, how he wanted to part.

He couldn't spin, pirouette or roll
She did a figure of eight as he fell in a hole.

Her tongue glided towards, what she thought was nice,
Instead to find frozen ice.

She thought he was going to be a six hero,
But ended up a big zero.

The seats walked off and boo
He was such a mood.

Leanne Tully (14)
Archbishop Ilsley RC School

MY LITTLE BROTHER

I have a little brother,
Who always makes a mess,
And when it comes to homework,
He couldn't care less.

My mom always tells him
To tidy up his room,
Instead he puts the tele on
And watches the cartoons.

When my dad tells him
To put away the ball,
He picks it up and plays with it,
And leaves it in the hall.

So when my gran comes for tea,
And has a nasty fall,
It's all because my little brother
Misplaced that ball.

Clare Fogarty (14)
Archbishop Ilsley RC School

THE PILL

Once a very long time ago,
There were three boys I used to know
They always used to say to me,
I wonder how taking drugs would be?
Then one day they had some pills,
That they said gave you some great thrills
I said no, I don't know why
I guess I did not want to fly
But they took the pill
Got the chill
Flew so high
They touched the sky
Now fifteen years on I look at them and see
Who I would be
If I had said yes,
And took the pill
Which gave the thrill
I know that I would not be flying
Right now I would probably be dying.

Aiden Teague (14)
Archbishop Ilsley RC School

THE DAY I MISSED THE BUS

I was just getting ready for school,
I had just put on my tie.
I peered through the window,
To see the bus go by.

I cursed till I ran out of words,
In fact I almost cried.
I stepped into the rain,
I muttered and I sighed.

I walked to the bus stop
I then put on my hood.
A speeding car splashed me,
I knew this day wouldn't be good.

Then, finally, the bus arrived,
I didn't know which bus it was,
I didn't really care.
I wanted to get out the rain,
I hoped it would take me there.

The doors opened and so I asked,
'Will this take me to the Green?'
I looked around for companionship,
No friends were to be seen.

The driver smiled and politely said,
'Yes my boy it surely will.'
I was overwhelmed and extremely chuffed.
I was so happy I had a thrill.

I was terribly late,
I ran up to the bolted gate.
I wondered what's happening today?
I then remembered it was teacher training day.

David Cox (13)
Archbishop Ilsley RC School

THE SNOWMAN

The snow is falling thick and fast
How much longer will it last?
Children with their hats and scarves
Having fun and lots of laughs
Let's build a snowman one child said
And stick a hat upon his head
Stones for eyes, a carrot for its nose
And little sticks for snowman toes
And in the morning when it's still cold
We'll find a coat that's very old
To wrap the snowman to keep him warm
'Cause we've been told there is a storm
We have to go now, the weather's worse
The weather wizard has said its curse
I hope the wind doesn't blow you away
We've worked so hard we want you to stay
So please Mr Wind, don't be bad,
And make all these children very sad
The snowman is a very good friend
And we don't want our friendship to end
The night is here and it's time for bed
So we'll say goodnight and rest our heads
The morning breaks we awake from our sleep
And all that's left are the clothes in a heap
The snow has stopped, the wind has gone
And Mr Snowman couldn't stay on
He's moved on and made new friends
And all his love the snowman sends
So don't be sad or start feeling blue
'Cause in your heart he'll always be with you.

Joseph Skerrett (11)
Archbishop Ilsley RC School

THE BIG FIGHT LIVE

In the blue corner stands me all alone
In the red corner stands the world on its throne
As it takes a giant leap for mankind
In my discoveries I finally find
Voices shouting 'Set me free'
They haven't had time to look and see
I move fastly
It follows me
With its consistency
To beat me down to the ground and to
Put a tax on every pound.
And now I have finally found
The world has come to drown.

Christopher Smith (14)
Archbishop Ilsley RC School

SPAGHETTI JUNCTION

Around and around,
In and out,
Cars and lorries move about.
Up and down at a tremendous rate,
On the junction that looks like spaghetti on a plate
Lights flashing,
Rain splashing,
Speeding round a bend.
Driving faster on the road that seems to never end.

Anthony McVay (13)
Archbishop Ilsley RC School

TRAVELLING TO SPACE

Travel through space to the stars
Travel to Jupiter, Saturn and Mars
Travel with aliens, they're green with one big eye
But they are friendly, I wouldn't lie.
We fly in a rocket going very fast
Looking out the window, planets zoom past.
Their language is hard to understand
We use signs with our hand.
'Asteroid' the aliens said.
'Bang' the rocket crashed, I banged my head.
I'm not hurt, I'm just in shock,
'Jay' Mom's shouting 'Turn off that alarm clock'.

Jay Yeomans (11)
Archbishop Ilsley RC School

MY SCHOOL

My school is such a bore,
But isn't everyone's?
They tell you off for everything you do,
'Don't shout, don't scream whatever you do,
Or there will be a detention for you.'
'Do your homework, do your work, don't talk!'
Is there anything you can do without getting told off?
And of course not letting the children call you a boff!
'Don't run, don't skip, don't hop, don't even breathe,
You little horrid child don't even sneeze!'

Rachael Pinson (12)
Archbishop Ilsley RC School

FRIENDS

F ind a person.
R eally get to know them by,
I ntroducing yourself.
E njoy the moment.
N ow ask the person to go out.
D o things with them that you never thought you could ever do
S oon you will be friends.

Friends are special things that you keep close
You treasure a friend forever.
A friend is like keeping a pet. Sometimes you can play with it for hours,
Then again there are times when you could just throw it away.
Think of a friend as a relative not a person.
Not a thing you use to catch the bus with just so you don't look like a
loner.
Not someone you use to carry your bags.
This friend should be one of the closest relatives to you
The first person you should invite to a sleepover is your friend
The first person I thought about inviting to Alton Towers, for the
weekend is my best friend.
A friend should respect you and you should respect them.

In future years you will most probably separate and see less of each
other.
This don't mean never talk to each other.
My father has been a friend with his mate for thirty-five years.
He is forty-one.

Kieran Hannon
Archbishop Ilsley RC School

LIFE'S REALITIES

Out on the streets, people having fun
Until some mad person pulls out a gun
You get popped in the head
And then you are dead.

You don't know what's happened until it's too late
Then by the trigger you discover your fate.

It could have happened to anyone but,
It happened to you
So you've got to ask yourself one question
What did you do?

There is no answer, for you to find
In the back of your blank dead mind.

And now you're dead
But you should have stayed in bed
Your life's done and dusted
But the guy never got busted.

If you face the reality
There will be fatality.

It's hard to believe what can be done
All by the power of a little object called

The gun.

Jamie Nolan (14)
Archbishop Ilsley RC School

HIGH

I am the poet of perfection,
My eyes bright as the moon, looking down on the darkness below me,
My heart is a half full glass, to someone else it's half empty,
My smile is wide as a fat person, eating up the glory,
My mind is working overtime, I haven't had a break yet,
My confidence is high as Mount Everest, I don't want to climb down.

I feel like something, in a world of somebodies
I'm as confident as a boxer, knocking out my troubles,
I'm as popular as a film star, everywhere I go I hear a hello,
I am a wheelie bin, disposing of my downfalls.

I am the president of providence, protecting my place,
I am the florist of fulfilment, arranging my success.

I won't be the dustman of dependence, talking trash.

Paul Dillon (14)
Archbishop Ilsley RC School

PUSSY, PUSSY

Pussy, Pussy where are you?
Pussy, Pussy down the loo.
Pussy, Pussy I should smack your paw,
Pussy, Pussy you broke your cat law,
Pussy, Pussy you're only seven,
Pussy, Pussy you've gone to Heaven,
Pussy, Pussy could have saved you,
Pussy, Pussy didn't want to.

Simon Brooke (12)
Archbishop Ilsley RC School

THE GHOST THAT HAUNTS US

You hear a noise in the night
You're scared it gives you a fright.

You creep downstairs to see what it is
Everyone is asleep plus the dog Liz.

You hear a bang you are scared
You see a sign floating saying 'Beware!'

You jump on the sofa you look around
Suddenly everything is quiet you can't hear a sound.

You see something white whoosh past your head
You jump upstairs into your bed.

You wait a minute you come from under the cover
Then you run like the wind to tell your mother.

'You're having a bad dream go back to bed'
'The ghost is waiting' I said.

I crept into my bedroom as quietly as I could
The ghost was waiting for me as I knew he would.

'Don't hurt me, don't put me in the black sack.'
He went away and never came back.

Jade Carr (11)
Archbishop Ilsley RC School

MAD DAD

To me of all people
Why did he do it?
I tried to help him,
With me he'd get through it.

He didn't want me,
Nor any of my help,
I was fooled all along,
It wouldn't work out.

He carried on boozing,
Playing his game,
Hurting those who loved him,
Oh what a shame.

His violence and anger,
Affected all those around,
My mum was left hurt
Lying on the ground.

He thought he was tough,
To fight with us girls,
Making us weep
And tugging our curls.

Enough was enough,
We all moved right away,
His mind-twisting games,
Weren't convincing us to stay.

His body has grown weak,
Our lives can begin,
To help him now,
Would be a sin.

As we all now know,
Never again
Will Mad Dad
Be fighting to win.

Denise Ward (15)
Archbishop Ilsley RC School

FOOTBALL MAD

Football, football,
That's what I like,
Kicking the ball,
And scoring goals!

Goal, goal, everywhere!
But the referee needs some glasses,
Ref, ref get some glasses,
The fans are getting so, so mad!

Goal, goal, it's a goal!
Now that's gonna put them,
Up in the tables,
Just one more goal will separate it.

Goal, goal, that will do it!
Here we go, we're going up!
There's the whistle, 2 - 0!
Yes, yes, we're all glad!

Now we need to continue like that,
Goals, goals, goals,
And up, up, up,
Three points for us!

Matthew Hardwick (11)
Archbishop Ilsley RC School

THE BULLY

He is the minister of madness,
The baron of badness,
The king of cruelty,
He is a bully,
He is my bully.
His fists are a full deck of cards,
Which he deals to me for the sake of being,
His heart is a cold, hard iron,
Which he releases to me, for being irritating he says
I feel like a man lost in the desert,
Lonely and deserted
I am the soldier of solitude,
I am the slave of sadness
But soon I will be the victor of vengeance.

James Hopkins (15)
Archbishop Ilsley RC School

DOWN, DOWN, DOWN

Ten minutes left, Man Utd down
Down, down, down in the Vauxhall Conference
Playing the likes of Hereford and Woking
Man Utd score it's now 2 - 2.

Five minutes left, the ref gives a pen.
A hooligan comes on and kills the poor ref.
Blood spilling everywhere, Rodney takes the pen.
Slipping and sliding the ball rolls in.

Two minutes left, Beckham snaps a twig,
Off he comes and on comes the missus.
Dancing seems very useful
As she dazzles her way, to make the long ball.

Extra time comes, Fergie blows his nut
He storms off steaming with envy
Ten seconds left, Rodney scores again
They think it's all over,
It is now.

Sean Mulcahy (11)
Archbishop Ilsley RC School

THE CHRISTMAS POEM

Christmas is coming,
The rain is falling.

Tip, tap, tip, tap goes the rain,
On the window pane.

The pavement is slippy, watch out
Don't fall,
It's the most important day of all.

We cannot wait for this day to come,
So Grandad can open his bottle of rum.

It's Christmas Eve no one's around,
No one is making a sound.

In the morning I shall wake,
To shake my mom and dad awake.

It's going to be the best Christmas ever!

Laura Kilroy (11)
Archbishop Ilsley RC School

PREHISTORIC PARENTS

If it's not your parents acting annoying
They're acting too old.
All they do is shout and scream,
And say 'Do as you're told!'

If you want to go out
They say 'Tidy your room'
You laugh at the idea
Of using a broom.

When they tell you off for telling lies,
You try to explain it's the truth in disguise
But when you tell the truth you still can't win,
They're still convinced you're drowning in sin.

They say they love you,
But you feel no trust,
Because they think you live
In a world of lust.

They don't realise how the world has changed
From when they were born in the stone-age!

Katie Lindsay (13)
Archbishop Ilsley RC School

THE BULLY

His eyes were as dark as coal, burning in my heart,
He is the devil of darkness
His heart is a broken window
I wish I could break him into tiny pieces.

When he punched me I went red like a tomato,
I couldn't face anyone
It was like a box of fists packing my pain
Eventually after I was so hurt, he walked off.

I felt so afraid, not knowing where he would be next,
I felt so sad
Tears ran down my face as fast as a cheetah
Cuts and bruises covered my face like a rash.

I am the loner of loneliness and
The dog owner of disaster and depression
Soon I will seek revenge over the barrister of badness
You'll see.

Stuart Bartlett (14)
Archbishop Ilsley RC School

POEM WITH ATTITUDE

Come on, try it, it's just a laugh,
Yeah funny ha, ha stop being daft,
Don't be a wimp, it won't do you any harm
Okay! If you say so, but I won't be taking part.

But it's an experience I would recommend
Everyone to have,
Why? So they can kill off brain cells they need
It makes you feel so high you can touch the sky,
Well I'll take a rain-check I'm scared of heights.

What you're afraid of is taking a chance,
You're boring and square. . .
Is that supposed to hurt me and make me take part
No I'm just finally saying what I feel in my heart,
Well if you feel that way I'll get some new mates.

Before I go though let me just say,
You may feel big and clever getting high,
But let me tell you something, carry on and you'll soon die.

Rebecca Eschoe (15)
Archbishop Ilsley RC School

ANGER

Why me?
Can't anyone see,
I'm dying from the inside,
I don't mind school,
It's the people I don't like.

Nasty people bossing me around,
Causing trouble,
Arguing the toss,
Punching me when I'm down,
Never helping me up.

Friends, who needs them?
Well I do,
If only someone would stand up for me,
What a dream a life with love in it
Don't get me wrong my family is great.

But people at school get me down,
Down in the dumps,
But I'll be all right in the end,
I'm stronger than them,
I will not let them beat me.

I just can't let them win,
I can't.

Helen Armstrong (14)
Archbishop Ilsley RC School

DAMN DA MAN IS FINE!

Met him at a party,
The lights bouncing off his face,
Looked at my girls,
Said 'Damn da man is fine!'

Saw him standing by the bar,
Cool as all the drinks in it,
Winked at me with those sexy eyes,
'Damn da man is fine!'

Made his way across the dance floor,
Eyes constantly on the prize,
Reached me and pulled my waist to his,
'Damn da man is fine!'

I looked at him, he looked at me,
Both breathing intense and heavily,
Inhaled, exhaled, closed our eyes and kissed,
'Damn da man is fine!'

Everybody flocked to see,
This fine looking man standing with me,
One cheeky girl still asked him to dance,
Said, 'Nah, this man is mine!'

Reaha McLarty (14)
Archbishop Ilsley RC School

PEER PRESSURE

They laugh; I weep
They taunt; I threat
On the battlefield the righteous stand
On the playground they fall
Sticks and stones will break your bones
The edifice will crush you!

Yes, the edifice, damnation
A peer of demolition
No, is the chant of the righteous
No, is the chant of the oppressed
Sticks and stones will break your bones
The edifice will crush you!

Yes, the edifice, persecution
A peer attacking the proud
A group; aspirations a diktat, thou Bolshevik are they
Communists in their views; dictated are they
Sticks and stones will break your bones
The edifice will crush you!

Yes, the edifice, predators
A peer led by a scavenger
One creates the views - the dictator
One shares the views; no separate stratagems . . . no persecution
Sticks and stones will break your bones
The edifice will crush you!

Their pressure is stolid
My contempt is greater still . . .
I stand; they fall.

Joseph Murray (15)
Archbishop Ilsley RC School

STICKS AND STONES

What did I do to deserve all of this?
The punches,
The kicks,
The shower of fists.

Sticks and stones will break my bones,
And words will always hurt me.

The taunting,
The bruising,
It tears at my mind,
Your insults get stuck in my teeth as they grind.

Sticks and stones will break my bones,
And words will always hurt me.

Even if I run,
I know you will find me.

And now I'm gonna end it,
Now I'm gonna take the hit,
Now I'm gonna leave it all,
Now I'm gonna take the fall.

Sticks and stones will break my bones,
And words will always hurt me.

I hope you're happy you have won,
I hope I haven't stopped your fun,
I hope you still have your self-esteem,
I hope I haven't spoilt your dream.

Not sticks and stones
Or
Words of hate
I did it all myself.

Peter Murtagh (15)
Archbishop Ilsley RC School

A TEENAGE LOVE STORY

His name was Damon
Brown hair and blue eyes
He had a stutter and a lisp
And lips every girl wanted to kiss.

In the playground he stared at me
I saw 'cos I couldn't stop staring at him
He brushed passed me at every chance
I thought this was the start of romance.

Thinking of him gave me butterflies
And his face permanently occupied my mind
He said he'd kiss me at the party tonight
It felt as though I'd been waiting all my life.

Well, at the party I did kiss him,
But so did Jodie, Tracy and Lisa
The tears stung the edges of my eyes
I ran into the toilets and I cried.

I heard the door open and I hid my face
I didn't want anyone to see me cry over a boy
A soft hand lifted my chin
I stared into big blue eyes, it was him.

He told me he liked me best
He kissed the others to see if I cared
He said 'I love you.'
I said 'I love you too'.

Seven and a half months, we just split up
I'm too young for this kind of commitment
And this relationship lark
And anyway there's this new boy called Mark.

Chelsea Gaffey (14)
Archbishop Ilsley RC School

In The Playground

I walk into the playground
The same thing each day
A bully in the corner
Robbing someone's money
People playing football
A goal here and there
Future David Beckhams
Showing off their skills
Girls running around
Spreading rumours,
That are not true
Don't care who they hurt
They say it's only a joke
But sometimes it hurts
To hear people saying things behind your back
They don't know how this feels, *just!*
Because they have mates
I'm the one in the corner
Getting bullied each day
Never allowed to play football
They just push me away
This is what happens
Every single day
When I walk into the playground
The same thing happens
But this can't be stopped
I'm just simply too scared.

Ben Tranter (12)
Archbishop Ilsley RC School

FLINGS

Exams and studies and a little leisure
And that time we have for television
And socialising with our friends, but not until late
We have lots of time for all these tasks
Which make up our teenage lives
But some poor soul, always gets caught in a fling.

They become the fly getting caught in the web
Ready to be served on the spider's plate of passion
The red end of a bar magnet
Attracted to the pole of the direction you're heading in
The clock bares no relevance
Until the fling is flung.

Slowly you drift down a river, brimming its banks of friendship
And fly through the sky of cloud, the blue you set aside
Whilst you 'broaden' your horizon to one hundred and seventy five
degrees
From which one ray emits, just like your mind
As channelled as a tunnel and as convinced as a jury of soft hearts
Forgetting those you left behind.

As they look on, straining their eye sight
Their voices hoarse and as heard as a droplet in a disco room
Because of the impermissible -
Essence of '*Eternity*' alongside the rancidity of a rat
But in your mind everything is as fine as the felt
With which you wrote your own fate
But yet to come is the lesson, which cannot be taught
But only learnt

And the day you learn, strikes fire in your heart
A progressing operation of pain to your semi-conscious thoughts
A stampede of bewilderment crushing your awareness
Until it all boomerangs back and hits you
The fling is flung.

Richard Cox (15)
Archbishop Ilsley RC School

TEENAGE TROUBLES

Pu-ber-ty
The world alone frightens me
Your body changes, you grow hair,
It's a real shock, it's a real scare.

Why not get off with that girl?
Why not have an ecstasy pill?
In front ya mates for a joke,
Why not start to smoke?

Everyone picks on this boy,
Throwing him around like a toy.
You have to join yourself,
Scarring his heart with your mouth.

Back to getting off with that girl,
When your tongues touch it's a big thrill.
You slip away from your mates,
You do what she wants, whatever it takes.

A rollercoaster of emotions in just five years,
Now I can drive a car and drink beers.
All my mates are now couples
All of these are teenage troubles.

Andrew Bailey (14)
Archbishop Ilsley RC School

CONFORMING

Everyone was staring at me.
I couldn't say no
What would they think
If I didn't take it?
My fingers trembling, I took it.
I took one long puff
It wasn't as bad as all that
It just relaxed me, you know,
Calmed me down.
In fact, it was nice,
I enjoyed it.
And now everyone is my friend
It's great.
I'll only do it when I'm with them, though.
I'm still in control.
Now I'm doing I can't stop
I spend all my spare money on it.
I can't live without it.
I take other stuff now as well
Anything I can get my hands on, really
Everyone does
I've become one of them
I try not to think about tomorrow.
Tomorrow, I could be dead
Oh well, at least I'm popular.

Daniel Tolster (14)
Archbishop Ilsley RC School

TWELVE WAYS OF LOOKING AT A BASEBALL

An orange jumping across the road.
Loadsa little oranges jumping across the road.
A happy pumpkin at Hallowe'en.
A fairground ride spinning for as long as it can.
A disco ball spinning showing oranges.
A shameless tramp getting pushed around.
A hard head with nothing known as a brain.
A little cannibal getting slammed by giants.
A missing body part sitting in the corner.
A peach lost in the thorns ready to die.
A tangerine in World War II with the floor.
A kumquat headbutting the blue trampoline.

Terence Ryan (12)
Archbishop Ilsley RC School

POEM ON CRIME

Crime is a thing which happens today
Everyone goes the wrong way
I hate walking round by myself
I may know the good guys and the bad guys,
But I'm still alone.
Bad things happen everyday
There's never any good news
I hate fights, racism, drugs and physical stuff.
I hate crime
Put a stop to it, now!

Elouise Teeling (14)
Archbishop Ilsley RC School

IN THE QUEUE

I was standing in the queue that day
I smelt that smell I always smell
Hot dogs, sausage rolls, burgers and chips
Those things I look forward to every day
Tasty, tasty, burgers and chips
Money ready in my hand
Only five more people to go
No! Only one burger left
Next please,
Next please,
Three to go, two to go
Oh, no he took it!

Shane Austin (13)
Archbishop Ilsley RC School

THE PAIN OF AGONY

Conflict is like a living hell,
You can't get away from it,
It's like a deep, descending black well,
My fear betrayed my quivering lip.

I look sharply around at the sorrowful eyes
Glimmering in the disgusting pain
People pass the book on and don't take the hard truth, blame
Conflict is like a living hell,
You can't get away from it,
Try to stop it and the agony will swell.

Aarron Wynne (13)
Bishop Challoner RC School

WAR, WAR, WAR

Why is there war?
Is it because people think that they will gain?
All it does is make people's minds and hearts sore
It makes us all grieve in pain.
As the war comes near to an end
All the people dance and sing
The countries become real good friends
And the towns make the bells ring
The funerals are held for the men that battled
It was as if after fifty years
The people down the road heard the war, they always hear
All they heard was the guns that rattled and tattled
Here's the end of my poem
I was inspired by Wilfred Owen.

Ryan Wilson (13)
Bishop Challoner RC School

ALONE

In the dark, in a corner her eyes begin to swell
As the river flows her thoughts are broken
The cries of the children's laughter are like
Sirens to her ears.
The sun is overtaken by the clouds and
Lightning strikes twice,
Her smile too shy to make an appearance is
Taken for granted much like her tears
The lightning only laughs and the light too far to listen
Her faith is weak, much like herself,
Her confidence was shattered
Now all she has are her tears, in a corner in the dark.

Clara McDonald (13)
Bishop Challoner RC School

CONFLICT

The atmosphere so cold and tense
As one by one they hit the ground
The war so bloody, have they no sense?
The monstrous guns produce that harsh, harsh sound,
Their faces so pale like the snow on a winter's day
The deadly silence was interrupted by their first cry
Who will move these dead people in the way?
As the mourning comes to an end, someone lets out a sigh
The friends stand there with thoughts in their minds
Who shall notice when they're not around
Because they're dead on the ground.
It's finished for the day as the shadow makes me blind
The war is over along to see
He shall be waiting at home for me.

Elisha Rogers (13)
Bishop Challoner RC School

MY CONFLICT POEM

There was a war, a terrible war,
There was a lot of people who wanted to fight
It was the worst thing people saw,
As they were fighting, it was a horrible sight.
You could hear the straining noises of the guns
And the crashing of bombs and the grenades,
The grenades wailed above the sound of guns
The sound of the bombs were worse than the grenades.

The planes were dropping bombs everywhere
The ground was littered with dead bodies
The bombs were being dropped on the bodies
Bombs crashed here, there, everywhere,
The fighting never stopped at night
It was a frightening sight.

Joe Baker (13)
Bishop Challoner RC School

SILENT TURNS

What a night,
As silent as can be
Not even a star shining -
There's no one out to see
The silent breaks,
We all wait underground.
The land starts to shake,
Can you hear that sound?

Bang! Bang! Bang!
There it goes again
That loud tune replaying in our heads
Bang! Bang! Bang!
The sounds of screams fill the air with fear
I long to go home to be with my dear.

Corrine McKeown (13)
Bishop Challoner RC School

BOYS IN WAR

When the shot is fired they fall into filth and mud,
Then they're forgotten like a leaf fallen from a tree
Except when they fall, the ground is soaked in human blood,
While those at home wait for news from over the sea.

Thousands of boys were sent to be killed,
And those who escaped would be made lame
And the families of boys whose blood was spilled,
Would rarely ever be the same.

Boys grew up away from home,
Women saying 'It's for the best,'
But no knowing when they felt alone,
And not knowing when they had come to rest.

The mustard wars will never come around,
But cyber wars, well they haven't been drowned.

Eve Tarpey-Vickers (13)
Bishop Challoner RC School

WAR

The banging of the guns was the song for the dead,
Every minute, every hour, ever day
When they looked at the dead, 'Oh another one' they said.
They only had a bit of time to pray
People were stabbed and all you heard was screams
You could hear the bullets coming out of the gun
It was like everyone had horrible nightmares or dreams,
And the killing won't stop until they're done.

Everyone was terrified of being shot,
All their family and friends would be killed
They wished it would stop they'd be really thrilled
But they know that it would not
You could see the children crying without their mums,
And they are scared of the sound of the big and loud guns.

Sundip Nandera (14)
Bishop Challoner RC School

BATTLE

War is a battle,
War is a contest,
City kids go live with farmers and their cattle,
This war would be the longest.

Many people died,
Many people suffered,
Many people lied,
Many people were undercover.

Men went to war,
Woman stayed behind,
It was the law,
The men didn't mind.

War is wrong,
Wars last long.

Majid Ali (14)
Bishop Challoner RC School

THE BEAUTIFUL GAME

Why do those fans show the ref such hate?
So what if the player dived a fake
Those fans shout abuse in this big debate
Every ref can make a mistake.

The ref pointed to the spot as his final decision,
Those fans bellowed their anger and remorse,
The ref said the players made a collision,
Those fans were now to use force.

Lighters and bottles were thrown onto the game,
The winning team could not wait for the end,
Just five minutes for them to defend,
Now those fans had one man to blame.

At last the final whistle came,
And that was the ugly side of the beautiful game.

John Biggs (14)
Bishop Challoner RC School

THE WARS

These wars are violent and full of blood,
Young boys forced into battle,
In the trenches there is a flood of mud
The dead get trampled on by soldiers as cattle
Cover up your head there's flying lead,
If you get hit you're going to die
Soldiers don't get to sleep on beds
All around you screeching grenades fly.

Dead people lie in the mud,
Skin paler than white
All soldiers full with fright
Around the bodies just mostly dried up blood
Soldiers become blind, death and dead,
Then the soldiers end the war
When the captain has lost his head.

Kieran Jeffrey (14)
Bishop Challoner RC School

LOST PETALS

Bang! Crash! Bang!
Boom!
The sound of another town being bombarded.

Boom!
Many more people have departed.

Smack! Boom!
Boom!
There's another one,
Off we trot to the shelter room,
Just think another town, gone
But wait, a moment's hush.

Wallop!
Boom!
Boom!
And off go the soldiers, all in a mad rush.

And as dusk settles, another flower loses all its petals.

Stefan Reidy (13)
Bishop Challoner RC School

UNTITLED

Kaboom! Kaboom!
The brave soldiers threw their grenades
Bang! Bang!
The bullets go flying piercing everything
Ahh, ahh!
The screams of agonising pain, then quiet,
Silently, softly, they die.
Trumpets play with wailing sounds,
The chaos, yell and scream
Life ends as the loved ones
Are lost and missed.
Once again the battlefield is
The cemetery for those who die
At war
The cemetery for the brave.

Robert Rumney (13)
Bishop Challoner RC School

WARS

Wars are dangerous, bloody and brutal,
People fight for right over wrong,
For what they believe in life is crucial
But people die like heroes unsung.
They lie in the trenches, their eyes not blinking
Bullets are flying, that piercing lead
They followed their orders blindly not thinking
They fought to be free but now they are dead.

Although people die, others will live
Mothers will weep for sons they have lost
In young men's lives they are counting the cost,
For man to be free their lives they will give
Why can't there be peace?
Why doesn't war cease?

Joseph Knight (13)
Bishop Challoner RC School

THE GRUESOME RIOT

Crash! Bang! The riot had begun
Chairs and brutal blows were being launched
At fans' faces as the screams of terror ran through the ground.

Snooker balls and snooker cues were being shredded
On fans' eyes and heads,
While blood and guts filled the air.

The bone-chilling noises surged through
People's bodies while people were getting
Killed,
As if nothing mattered.
For some could cry from lost relatives
But others could not for they had no eyes.

While children watched people's lives being flushed down the drain.

James Hanlon (14)
Bishop Challoner RC School

FOOTBALL HOOLIGANS

The match was over, the score was 2 - 0
The riots started before the whistle was blown
By the sound of the crowd, they were ready to kill
They invaded the pitch and bottles were thrown
Security urgently calling for back-up
It was getting out of hand. Someone was going to get hurt
The referee lay there, beaten up
Another man lay there, dead, in a football shirt.
Kicks and punches at every direction
I was surprised, I'd never seen this before
In a match against Everton and Liverpool
Then there was a loud sound like a gun
A man was shot in the head
Now he's dead.

Sean Dineen (13)
Bishop Challoner RC School

THE FEAR OF WAR

In the war the guns rule,
Every day is a nightmare
It's an on going duel,
People die everywhere
Grenades landing,
Food running out
Hearing the banging
Hopes mounting.

Families crying,
Hiding in trenches,
Tears fall from wenches,
Hoping their son is not dying
Very quick funerals,
No time for burials.

Yanik Sookloll (13)
Bishop Challoner RC School

NOT SO PERFECT!

Hitler wanted total power,
To other countries he would scour.

Across sea and land his armies would file,
The dead and grieving began to pile.

Every night the sound of screams,
Shattered a million people's dreams.

Mothers losing their cherished sons,
In the blink of an eye, one shot of a gun.

Murdered for being Catholic, Gypsy or Jew,
All they wanted was the *perfect* you!

Blond hair, blue eyes every one the same,
They judged you and they didn't even know your name.

Rachel Smith (13)
Bishop Challoner RC School

CONFLICT

When people do not agree
Then rows will surely follow
And conflict this will surely be
Screaming, shouting, trouble
Disagreements loud and clear
Through the open window pane
Sometimes the whole street must hear
Hopefully most of us are sane.

But for some there is no peace
Quiet times not known to them
This would be such a gem
For the arguments would cease
Oh for the peace of mind
That comes from someone being kind.

Josef Yazigi (13)
Bishop Challoner RC School

THE TRENCHES

The trenches wet, soggy and brown
My feet cold, my toes numb
Most of the people shot down
But I'm not dumb
It's no pellet gun my son,
These guns are not for fun
The wails of fear heard all around
While the gunshots surround.

The Germans shot us like falling weights
I think we should think of our lovers
And the others
But the only person we hate is hate
The sound has gone our heads hang
For one person has just went
Bang!

Gary Smith (13)
Bishop Challoner RC School

SIBLINGS

My brother really is a pain
He's tall and slim with short blond hair
He thinks he's cool, I think he's vain
We really are an argumentative pair
Sometimes we fight and argue loud
No one wins, things just run dry
No sorrys pass, we're both too proud
We walk away with our heads held high.

It could be worse I'm not sure how
Maybe we could really dislike each other
No I couldn't, he's my brother
He's not too bad, he's OK now,
I'm not mad, it's you, you're insane
Oh no it's started all over again.

Kirsty Trewerne (13)
Bishop Challoner RC School

A SONNET OF CONFLICT

It's a time of pain when there is conflict and war,
People are dying of hunger and thirst
Many lives are devastated and many people are sore,
I wonder who started this bloody trend first?
The air is gloomy and there is no sign of the sun,
It's now a ruin, where the cattle once dwell
Children are crying as they aimlessly have to run
This is the sad story which one could ever tell
The food supplies are short and there is nothing in the store,
So vicious are such horrid days,
The community is shattered with dead bodies lying on the floor
The scenery is ugly covered with smoke and haze
When I bow my head and
To God I pray
I hope such evil days never ever stay.

Qasim Shah (13)
Bishop Challoner RC School

HELL ON EARTH

They met in stifled air,
The firing line is set,
The guns rage with rampant flare
Then the oppositions met
The pride of men shines their soul,
The men are weak, flustered, worn
Their grave is but a muddy hole
Their hopes of a glorious war are torn.

Their bed is just a muddy pit,
The only music they hear is an assembly of guns
Bullets pile up by the tons,
Their lives could be over in one small hit
While they wait for screams and crying
All they hear is bombs flying.

Charlotte Roberts (13)
Bishop Challoner RC School

WHAT IS WAR?

Were lives worth rushing?
Minds were distraught,
And the noise was deafening but wasn't forgiving
As innocent beings were caught
The moans of those who die
Is the smell of hate and fear where
Family and friends begin to cry
The fear is one not to bare.

The vision of hate rising
Is war which is not fair,
Then why should people care,
Because all we are losing are the lives of people dying.
What is war?
What is it good for?

Henry Kerali (13)
Bishop Challoner RC School

NO MORE WAR

The sirens have stopped,
No more guns,
All weapons are dropped,
Let's celebrate, have fun,
No more tears, no more screams,
No more funeral masses,
No more nightmares, no bad dreams,
No more choking gasses!

No more bodies on the ground,
No more blackouts,
No more horrible sounds,
No more help! Shouts,
No more tears,
And not so many fears!

Danielle Buswell (13)
Bishop Challoner RC School

FIGHTING

When people fight it makes my legs wiggle
I've seen the monstrous anger of one
And the other a big struggle
There is always a weaker one.

Scream and shout
Punches as fast as a gun
But the other still has to blow him out,
And all he can see is the shining sun.

Fast punch, fast kick,
He's up for anything
It makes me feel sick,
Seeing the other getting beaten up by
The fighting king.

One has been beaten up from
Head to feet,
Well the other is laughing with
His successful defeat.

Umar Zaman (13)
Bishop Challoner RC School

MAKE UP YOUR MIND!

What words can change your mind?
No word can change my mind,
Not even the birds' graceful song.
Maybe if you find the sweetest one.
Come on and meet this one then
But the moon is coming
Oh ok then 'ha, ha,' can't you beat that
It's out of tune!

Oh no the moon has fallen
'Shh' hear that, no listen then
Look up there at that owl's glistening eyes
Does that help your decision
I don't quite know
I bet you say no yep!
Oh no.

Fiona Ross (14)
Bishop Challoner RC School

WAR

People were called to the war
To fight for their country one for all
They said their goodbyes to them all
It was upsetting for them all
On a bleak night it all began
The soldiers were checking all the guns
The major's call had begun
To the tanks they had to run.

The war was deeply, exceedingly bad
The war brought destruction to them all
Some recovering forever more
Lots of people lost their dad
Most of the children were very sad
Some would never see their dad.

Bernard Ward (13)
Bishop Challoner RC School

THE WAR IS HORRID

The war is bad and brutal
The children so cold and frightened
The planes and bombs are flying
And death is in the air.

The ships are dropping one by one
People and their houses
The bullets are flying
And people are dying
Death is in the air.

Simon Holyhead (13)
Bishop Challoner RC School

MY DREAMS

These nuts that I keep in the back of the nest,
Where all my lead soldiers are lying at rest?
Were gathered in autumn by Nursie and me
In a wood, a well, by the side of the sea.
This whistle we made
How clearly it sounds
By the side of a field at the end of the grounds
Of a branch of a plane with a knife of my own,
It was Nursie alone.
The stone with the white and yellow and grey
We discovered I cannot tell how far away
And I carried it back although weary and cold
For though Father denies it
I'm sure it is good.

Jodie Colley (12)
Colmers Farm School

A SAD LITTLE BOY

I will tell you a story of a little sad boy
Who was always picked on and never had joy
No sun was rising for this little boy who wished
For happiness to come.
But it never came, till one happy day
When his mother gave birth to a little boy
Who he can play with and love for life to come
And never have doubt for everything to come.

Adam Jones (12)
Colmers Farm School

SCHOOL DAYS

School's an education
You'll enjoy it if you try,
The uniform is really bad
It makes you want to cry,
The rules are pretty scatty
Whoever made them up,
Teachers always say
We cannot wear make-up.
Three lots of homework a day
Course work to fit in as well,
I thought school finished
When they rang the bell.
Monday morning comes too soon
Maths is always first,
Graphics, Spanish, PE's fine
Science is the worst!

Amanda Needle (14)
Colmers Farm School

MY FAMILY

My mom buys me chocolates
My dad buys me clothes
My brothers buy me nothing
Until I tidy up their room.

My nan and grandad buy me anything
My auntie buys me shoes
My cousin is so sweet and all I can say
Is my family is so neat.

My brothers love partying
They think they are cool
The teachers thought they were quiet
While they were at school.

I myself am different
I think that I am the best
But my mom and dad love all of us
We often put them to the test.

Lisa Whitehouse (12)
Colmers Farm School

WET BREAK

Ten minutes early the bell goes
All I can hear is lots of moans.
Teacher announces 'It's wet break'
The girl next to me says 'Goodness sake!'
'Don't stop, carry on, wait till the second bell has gone' my head rings
'Bring! Bring!' The bell sings
'Hurry! Hurry!' It's play!'
Melissa recaps her make-up
While the teacher sips from a cup.

I look out the window rain
What a pain
A flood is starting outside the labs
While across the playground runs Richard Gabs
I rummage through my bag for crisps
But all I can find is two chocolate dips.

Two minutes later the bell goes
Now all I can hear is lots of groans!

Jessica Rogers (11)
Colmers Farm School

TEST

It's a four-lettered word that everybody hates,
Especially me and all of my mates!
My teacher says 'It's time for a test!'
I feel like saying 'Oh give it a rest!'
As she slowly and carefully passes out the test sheets,
Everybody starts quivering in their seats
I start to get sweaty palms
Though I know I must remain calm
I get the test sheet . . .
And my heart skips a beat.
I mean it's got $\frac{1}{2} + Y = X \div 2$ and that sort of stuff,
You know the algebra questions that are really tough
The hour passed by quick as a flash
And question six I still hadn't passed!
I knew I'd probably get nought,
And if I tried to cheat, probably get caught!
I know it is a stupid thing to do
But still I managed to signal my friend, Pat Gurew
'What's the answer to number four?'
But the teacher caught me and sent me out the door
Then she followed me out,
And began to shout something about
Me not being able to be trusted
Don't you just hate getting busted?
But I never really paid attention
So she said I had an hour's detention
So now it's a nine-letter word that everybody hates
And no one's more aware than me or my mates!

Carly McCormack (11)
Colmers Farm School

MY FIRST DAY AT SCHOOL

This school is so enormous,
It's bigger than I thought.
'The work is going to be hard!'
I hope I remember what I'll be taught
The first lesson starts in five minutes,
Everybody here seems so tall.
I feel like I'm going to get lost,
I feel so very small.
We've started the first lesson,
I don't know what to do
I smile at the girl next to me,
I wonder if she's scared too.
The bell has gone for dinner,
I think I'm getting to like it now
The teachers are so nice to me here,
They treat you older somehow.
Dinner time is over,
I am now in period four.
French is new to me,
But I like it best of all.
Today I've got two credits,
I think I've done really well.
I know my mom will be proud of me,
Oh, no it's time to go, I can hear the bell.
I love my new school,
It seems like I've been here forever
I've made lots of new friends today,
I hope this lasts forever.

Rochelle Peacock (11)
Colmers Farm School

WITHIN ME . . .

Who am I?
For I don't know
For that I look deep in my soul
The real me is . . .
I can be strong, I can be weak,
I can be wrong,
I like to seek and find out what
The world reveals
And what it hides
As I count the days
Which pass me by
And hear the heartless, tearless cries
The present, the future
I've yet to find,
The past's existence, I've left behind,
The last breath glows,
A second gone,
This is my poem, my life, is done.

Sandy Gordon (13)
Colmers Farm School

LUNCH

Ring, ring, ring goes the bell,
Line, line, line up in our lines,
Rush, rush, rush goes the pupils
Ready for our nice hot lunch.

Run, run, run in here we come,
Getting our plates all the while
And looking at lovely tasty food,
And pay, pay, pay to the lady.

Sit, sit, sit down at the tables,
Take our coats off to eat
Getting our knives and forks at the ready
We al eat, eat, eat!

James Wilkes (11)
Colmers Farm School

TEACHERS

Teachers, teachers,
Teachers, some are nice,
Some are just like Scary Spice
Teachers never learn,
They tell you off with pleasure,
Say the word, any word,
And you're sure to get a detention!

Now this is just the start,
Some get worse,
Some only have a first.

Now every class in the school
Has what we call a teacher's pet.
To us they are rats who should be taken to the vet!

Now let me tell you about the staffroom
These so called teachers
Have a hidden secret.
Why do the take sooo long to get to the door? And
Why do the say they are sooo poorly paid?

We should've definitely guessed it was the pest
The master of them all . . . the TV.

Kerri Dickens & Harriet Giles (11)
Colmers Farm School

HELL'S BELLS

The bell goes at 8.45
The children enter the classroom of Hell
As the teachers yell
'Sit down 7Z!' and the school stops dead because the teachers are off
Their heads!

The bell rings 'Oh!' the children shout
The door opens with a 'boom!' as they enter the classroom of doom!

The lessons start with a pound of the heart
They all shut up like the speed of a dart.

At the end of the day they all shout 'Yyyayy!'
And get ready for the next day!

Annabel Mawdsley & Nicola Kenney (12)
Colmers Farm School

WHAT ARE TEACHERS REALLY LIKE?

What are teachers really like when no one is around?
Do they pick their nose and eat it?
Do they spit on the ground?
I wonder what happens in their staffroom during lunch and break?
Do they have food fights using spaghetti and cake?
I bet our maths teacher hates being on a diet
Because when it's nearly lunch he always starts a riot.
Teachers are a mystery, I can't work them out.
Why do the job if all they do is shout?
No more teachers would mean no more school,
Everybody would be happy it would be cool!

Samantha Simmonds (11) & Sasha Casson (12)
Colmers Farm School

WAITING FOR BREAK TIME

The children push and shove,
The bell has already rung.
The children get in the classroom,
The door closes with a bang.
The teachers start talking,
And says his morning moan
'Test tomorrow' the teacher says
We all begin to groan.

The bell starts ringing again -
Now form period is done.
Maths is the first lesson,
Although it's not much fun.
Still looking at the clock now,
An hour has gone by
Still an hour left to break,
I let out a depressing sigh.

We run into the playground
We all scream and shout
At last our break is here -
It is now time to go out
I talk to my friends for a while,
Then I get something to eat.
I get a cake and a packet of crisps
And then try and find a seat.

Break has nearly finished -
Back to work oh well.
Break has gone so quickly
Off goes the bell.

Chloe Ainslie (11)
Colmers Farm School

MY LIFE

Every day I wake up to a row,
I get up, get dressed and ignore the terror
I get to school and see the smiling faces that greet me
Are they fake or sincere? Do they know me loud and clear?

They think I am a happy face
But I am a waste of space
When, oh when will they see that
Love is not a part of me?

My friends you know they just don't see
That life is just so hard for me
They love to work and play
But I can't wait to go away.

Some might think that I am thick
But they all just make me sick
Sometimes I just sit and sigh
But it is time to say goodbye!

Shannon Maynard (13)
Colmers Farm School

ALL ABOUT SCHOOL

The bell goes it's school time
How I hate that chime,
Teachers, teachers,
They're all little creatures,
They give us detention,
And other things I won't mention,
It's time for history
My isn't it a mystery
With all the times and dates.

It's time for lunch
All you can hear is crunch, crunch, crunch
Oh no, not French, nothing seems to make sense
Oh no, it's time to go home
I'll travel on the bus all alone.

Rebecca Williams (11)
Colmers Farm School

SCHOOL AIN'T COOL!

I was really looking forward to
Starting year seven. I wanted to
Achieve, learn and work hard.
Get loads of credits to fill my card.

The first few days I was quite scared.
But the teachers were nice, they really cared.
If we got lost they didn't mind
Friends would help, everyone was kind.

Geography, maths, science and DT many
Lessons they try to teach me,
French, history, and English, and in
Cooking I make a superb dish.

My best lessons are DT, history and maths
Break times are fun with lots of laughs.
For dinner I have sandwiches in the canteen
But they also make chips, sausages and beans.

I have now finished a term, nearly two
I know everywhere and the things I must do
But the best thing about school I really must say
Is that we're off on Saturday and Sunday.

Kera Bavington (11) & Louise Dipple (12)
Colmers Farm School

ENGLAND VS GERMANY

It stared off in '39 when Hitler took charge of the war
He had to be the most ugly man the world had ever saw,
So out came England the best army in the land
But I have to admit America gave us a hand
We won the war with strength and bravery
We really had to use our Navy.

Now to football of '66
You would think the match was fixed.
We won 4 - 2 with one dodgy goal
Without the likes of a goal king Cole
The World Cup trophy finally came to Wembley
Oh and apologies to China about your embassy.

Now to the last game at the Twin Towers
Soon to be closed within a few hours
We lost 1 - 0 to the German white
So we say to our Wembley, au revoir, goodbye and goodnight.

Martin Frost (14)
Colmers Farm School

DISASTROUS DINNERS

Here we go, hold on tight
Hungry bodies are in sight.
Smell the food, what's to eat?
Ouch! Somebody tramples on my feet.

Chatter, chatter who's next please?
Uuh! Look at the colour of the mushy peas
I'm getting closer, nearly there,
What shall I have? Do I dare!

What would you like? Came the voice
I think to myself nothing looks nice
Please can I have pizza and chips
Without the slimy gruesome dips?

I look at my meal, it doesn't look bad
If I could find a chair, I'd be glad.
Sat at the table I start to eat
Actually it's very nice, wow what a treat!

Jade Brooks (11) & Lara Keyte (12)
Colmers Farm School

STRANGE POEM

Disturbed by the chilling shiver
Running down my spine
I jumped straight to my window
Unaware of the time
Mom ran in 'What, what, what?'
'God knows but it has to stop!'

Three weeks running and still no improvement
It's all about my mind and its movement
A disturbance in the night with the images
Awakening me screaming it's just not right.

'Spoken to a doctor'
'No, there's no need'
People going crazy, strange indeed!

Toni Farrington (14)
Colmers Farm School

ALCOHOL ON WHEELS

Please don't drive when you've had a lot to drink,
Please just stop and try to think,
Of all the people that you will kill,
Just for a beer and a drive for a thrill.

It won't hurt to drink a lot less,
And it will keep you out of a mess,
So if you drink more and more,
It'll be the police that are knocking at your door.

So take this opportunity to think about your booze,
And think of all the things that you will lose,
Wife and kids whilst pulling skids,
Family and friends whilst speeding round the bends.

So please don't drink and drive,
And think of all the people that will still be alive.

Ashley Bird (15)
Colmers Farm School

A DAY AT SCHOOL

Early morning Science first,
The lesson that's apparently cursed,
Today we're studying Robert Turner,
The inventor of the Bunsen Burner!

Bell tones,
Walk up the stairs with aching bones,
To this lesson of maths,
We're using number paths.

Early lunch, whoopee!
I'll have some chips and a Slush Puppie
After lunch I've got DT
We're making rock cakes with kiwi.

My last lesson,
Who goes in the diary,
Sasha Casson,
She was naughty and rude to Sir,
So, he punished her.

Thomas Devaney (11)
Colmers Farm School

WINTER

Winter's here cold, very cold
No more hot sunshine
No more leaves left on the bare trees,
Yellow, green and red.

Frozen ponds and white snow.

People with gloves, scarves and woolly coats,
Makes you feel cold.
Blazing fires in houses,
Snug and warm.

Frozen ponds and white snow.

Crispy leaves on the ground,
Crunch, crunch, crunch.
Frost on the green grass,
Shiver, shiver.

Frozen ponds and white snow.

Emma Hake (12)
Colmers Farm School

LESSONS, LESSONS, LESSONS

School, school, school it makes me drool, drool, drool,
Lessons never end it just drives me round the bend,
They're really tiring and some of the teachers need firing.

> PE is so spacious and fun,
> All we do is dance, scream and run.
> Five periods of that would do me fine,
> PE is the lesson I want all the time.

Science is a good place for snoring,
Since it is so very boring
I wish that Science would give my a break
All that work we do gives me a headache!

> Break and lunch is the very best,
> After all we're not sitting a test
> But when break is over oh! For heaven's sake
> Maths is here another lesson I hate.

Now we get to hissssttttooooorrrryyyy and that's the lesson that lasts,
Since we're in the present but lingering on the past.

> Art is so lame and always a pain
> Draw, draw, draw is all we have to do
> We'd be better off sitting on the loo.

So there you have it that's what we think
Of all the lessons at school that really stink!

Kerrie Edge & Joanna Donnelly (11)
Colmers Farm School

ANOREXIA - WHY FAT IS GOOD FOR YOU

You hear it in the papers,
Another pop star being called 'fat' by the media
What is fat? Is it bad for you?
You feel sick.
You look in the mirror, check the scales
And you feel fat.

Nobody understands, but they say they care
How would they know what you think?
They can't stop you feeling fat.

Another girl dies tragically,
Starving herself.
She felt fat.

And you feel angry, lonely, depressed and used,
Like a pawn in a chess player's hand
They're crushing your heart and lungs - you can't breathe
There's a voice in your head, telling you it's wrong.
But you can't stop now,
It's a drug.
Your head is spinning. You feel dizzy.
They want to feed you, to make you eat
The mirror never lies.

You're getting thinner and thinner,
You're just skin and bones
Still, you're kidding yourself.

Your family and friends can't help you now,
You're sinking and sinking, the world is black.
Even now, you feel 'fat'.

Emily Thorpe (14)
Colmers Farm School

DETENTION, DETENTION

Detention, detention what's the point of it
Detention, detention I really hate it
Detention, detention you have it in class
Detention, detention because you drank a shandy bass.

D is for doing something wrong in class
E is for extra homework which I've done
T is for time spent after school
E is for an over excited child
N is for 'No' that teacher cried
T is for the thirty minutes after school
I is for I'm never doing this again
O is for 'Oh no' I've talked to my friend
N is for no not me again!

Matthew Naik (11)
Colmers Farm School

MY POEM

I could not think of what to write,
So thought I'd leave my paper white!
But as it got deeper into the night,
I thought of something I could write
My head was clear,
But my page was blank!
So I thought of a poem I'd heard before,
And I thought and thought,
But nothing came through,
So I thought that I'd leave it,
Up to you!

Lee McCartney (13)
Colmers Farm School

DON'T DO DRUGS

People tell me drugs are bad,
And you'd only take them if you were mad
I know Jim who takes those pills,
Just to feel these kind of thrills
He stopped having a wash
And lost all his dosh
So now he's a tramp on Cookie Street,
Getting his money by kissing feet,
If he doesn't stop he's going to die,
Just from pills which send him high
So if you are going to take some drugs,
Think about Jim and other thugs
Jim and his mates, just want to go high,
But surely soon they all will die.

Richard Kerrigan (13)
Colmers Farm School

DEAD END

'There is no way out' you said
'We're going nowhere fast
It's a cul-de-sac, it's finished
It's never going to last
We've hit a brick wall
It's the end of the line'
My eyes were filled with tears
'I thought we were fine . . .'

Zena Botfield (15)
Colmers Farm School

ANIMAL CRUELTY

Animals to human beings
Are stupid insignificant things
A new shampoo,
The latest spray,
Something to keep the germs away,
Are tested on these helpless creatures
By professors and their teachers.

People don't seem to understand
The pain they suffer that they can't stand.
The ordeal and anguish they go through,
Just imagine if it was me or you.
Some experiments go to their head,
And in the end they're relieved to be dead.

Michelle Wróblewska (13)
Colmers Farm School

THE DREAMCAST

I'm a Dreamcast
Soon I'll be a thing of the past
Like the Megadrive
No one will strive
To save my life
All the strife
I'll just have to admit what I am
Who would give a damn?
And soon I'll be dead!
Hidden forever, under the bed.

James Naik (13)
Colmers Farm School

ANIMAL CRUELTY SHOULD NOT BE HERE

Animals live everywhere
In our homes and on the streets
We keep our animals by our sides
As if they were our best friends.

But in a laboratory
Where they all wear white,
And everything smells so clean
There is a different story to it all.

Animals kept in cages
Petrified of everything that moves
Cages no simpler than a wire mesh
With no straw or bed, just solid metal.

But in the cages there is a fear
Of all the animals around them
They are all scared of what will happen to them next
But that's ignored all the time.

The scientists say that it is not harming them
But the animals cannot speak or express their feelings
So they could be suffering from depression
Or even stress.

Even if it helps our race for things like cancer and other drugs
But still there's no need for things like
Shampoo in their eyes when they don't have a way to take the pain
away
Hairspray up their noses to see if it's all right.

All this is wrong
But it still happens.

Peter Deacon (13)
Colmers Farm School

MY FAMILY

I love my family very much
Even when they get on my nerves
We often like to talk and discuss
About our boring day
The adults often about their jobs
I just sit back and think about
What I want to do when I'm older.
They try to make the decisions for,
What I'm gonna do when I'm older.
I know they want me to do the best
In life, they want me to learn from,
Their mistakes but I want to learn
Myself.
I wish I could just stay young.

Damion Gardner (13)
Colmers Farm School

THE TRAIN

Every night I hear the train
Huffin' puffin',
The steady beat of the wheels
Hitting the hot,
Grinding track.

Like a soldier drumming on
His drum,
The sound chugga,
Chugga, chugga,
Bang, bang, bang like a charging bull.

The beat stronger,
Approaching nearer, louder
The light has shone,
Quieter, quieter, quieter,
The sound has gone.

Nicholas Moorcroft (13)
Colmers Farm School

FOOTBALL WILL NEVER BE THE SAME

Football is all about money,
And most of it ends up in Ellis' tummy!
Players always demand high wages,
And demand their faces to be on back pages!
Why has Wembley been knocked down?
All that does is make me frown
Why knock down an historic place
When all it does is change it's face?
Players like Ronaldo are on ninety thousand pounds a week,
All this does is make the future of
Football look bleak
Some managers waste their cash,
On players who aren't very flash
Poor clubs like Halifax,
Are struggling to pay their weekly tax!
But richer clubs like Coventry City,
Will not take away the poor club's pity
They don't even donate ten grand,
For the club which soon will not have a stand
This is why we must act now,
Before the small clubs won't know how
As I'm coming to my final point,
I've got to go to dinner and have my juicy joint!

Scott Waldron (13)
Colmers Farm School

BIG RED MACHINE

If Stonehouse rocks my designed assault
I'm the Kronick at the bottom of a mindless thought
Psychotic over Kronick makes me rage in lust
Stomping all opposition till their brains are mashed
Seven foot three degree manic unseen can't nobody stop
The Big Red Machine?
I'm known as the king dead man walking
Fear no man and I live in a coffin
Look me in my eyes tell me what you see
King of the millennium and his name is me
Seven foot three first degree maniac unseen can't anybody stop
This Big Red Machine?

Andrew Poller
Colmers Farm School

KANE

He is over seven feet tall and flies like a plane
From the top rope.
His nickname is the Red Machine
He wipes every wrestler clean
He wears a red and black mask
And his face has never been seen
He has a brother called the Undertaker
The Choke-Slam is his finishing move
His favourite move is the Tombstone Pile-driver,
And is definitely the Red Machine.

Sam Lawrence (13)
Colmers Farm School

TRAPPED

In through the mouth and down
The throat I go,
I'm wearing a frown
Don't you know?

I've come to the lungs
I'm trapped inside
There's no way out
That's what I've cried.

With one mighty breath
There's a sigh of relief
As I go down to the liver
It looks like the Great Barrier Reef.

Bouncing on the kidney
I'm getting so high
It feels like
I'm about to fly.

Through the intestines
It's very sick
All the stuff in here
Is really thick.

Someone needs the toilet
God I may be free
All I have to do now
Is count 1 . . . 2 . . . 3 . . .

Joe Morrall (13)
Colmers Farm School

OUR FURRY FRIENDS

Clean, cuddly, tidy, nice and smooth
These are animals best kept at home.

Grumpy, lumpy, bumpy, rough and nasty,
Are animals best left alone.

Slimy, climby, dumb and dotty
Are but a few.

The snarly, humpty, greedy and heavy
Should all be kept in a zoo.

It's so well known that our furry friends
Could not survive without our human touch.
Ask yourself this, would we miss animals to love?
My answer is *yes*,
Ever so much.

Shelley Howard (13)
Colmers Farm School

CRUELTY

Here I am sitting in a cage
The handlers have no respect
I'm just a number on a page
All I do is just sit and reflect . . .

. . . on how humans test
On cats
Just to make themselves feel at their best
They also test on bats and rats.

Animals must have the right
Not to be tested on
They don't have the power to fight
If we don't stop now animals will be dead and gone.

Thomas Churchman (13)
Colmers Farm School

FOR OR AGAINST

Animals used in tests,
They just treat them as pests,
They don't get exercise
Big, small or any size.

People protest all the time
All marching in a straight line.
They shout and scream
It's a scientist's bad dream.

These animals are not pets
Looked after by technicians and vets
Just locked away in small cages
By scientists who get paid high wages.

But maybe it's not bad
We now have medicines we never had
Improving life for human kind
A real dilemma you might find.

This subject has its good and bad
But putting animals through pain is sad.
They are not allowed to have a choice
So people have become their voice.

Nicola Rose (13)
Colmers Farm School

LIFE IS A FLOWER

Life is a flower, waiting to burst,
Under the stars I wait to be heard,
Silence approaches as you are drawn near
Petals fall off like leaves on trees.

Life is a flower, waiting to jump,
We need to be strong just like a stem,
To protect us when we make mistakes,
We fall down when no one is there.

Life is a flower, waiting for water,
We need to have water, for our everyday needs,
We also need food and growth,
As we grow stronger we become much taller.

Life is a flower, it needs some space,
We all need space for our food to grow,
Space is when you need to be alone,
Peace and quiet can work wonders.

Life is a flower, it needs some love,
Everyone is happy, sadness is doomed forever,
Confetti is everywhere, someone has just got married,
This is the life, what do you think?

Elizabeth Curtis (13)
Colmers Farm School

TOO MUCH CRUELTY

Why do animal technicians treat me this way?
Because it's for humans health today,
And all this is mutating us
But are they bothered? No!

They stick us in small, cramped cages,
Because they don't want to spend their wages,
They test on us,
Because they're too much a wuss!

Why can't they leave us alone,
In our everyday lives,
Instead of stabbing us with knives,
And needles and much, much more!

Just because we are too weak,
Against the strong of the technician,
Doesn't mean that we don't have lives of our own,
And do they reward us with a bone? No!

Just because I'm a mutt,
Doesn't mean they can kick my hairy butt,
Can't they leave us alone
To carry on with our lives with a nice juicy chicken bone!

Craig Cumberton (13)
Colmers Farm School

JIM THE MAGICAL FISH

Jim the magical golden fish decided he would make a wish

He wished he could be a bird in the sky flying very, very high.
In the clouds above the crowds for everyone to see.

He wished he could be a leaf on a tree fluttering in the breeze
Showing off his autumn colours to everyone he sees.

He's sick of wishing, he wishes he was back in his bowl
Eating his food and chanting a song with bubbles.

Jessica Taylor (11)
Colmers Farm School

DRUGS

Drugs, drugs can make you high,
They can also make you die.
Don't smoke the draw,
'Cause it's against the law.
Don't take an 'E' they make you ill,
If you're not careful they can kill.
Don't snort crack, it gives you a buzz.
When you take a drug you start off high
Then you're on a low,
So don't touch a drug 'cause it's
Touch and go . . .

Daniel Caveney (13)
Colmers Farm School

MY HAMSTER BRITNEY

My hamster Britney is very cute
Her favourite food is definitely fruit.

She loves to go on her wheel
Which sometimes makes a squeal.

My hamster Britney is very small
But when she's on her feet she's very tall.

She has little beady eyes and
At night they sparkle with a surprise.

Her teeth are very long
And very, very strong.

She's always standing on her feet
Which are very small and sweet.

Charlotte Green (11)
Colmers Farm School

MATHS POEM

Maths is easy,
Maths is hard
Just pick up your pen and try very hard
You never know when you'll be wrong
So give it a try you might just be right.
So why don't you try with all your might.

Rameena Nagra (11)
Colmers Farm School

MY HAMSTER CHUCKIE

My hamster Chuckie is brown and white,
My hamster likes to play all night.

My hamster Chuckie runs in his ball,
He likes to run up and down the hall.

My hamster Chuckie is really sweet,
My hamster has little pink feet.

My hamster Chuckie makes a noise,
When he plays with all his toys.

Sophie Yardley (12)
Colmers Farm School

MY DOG

My dog's called Max
He likes to relax
In front of the fire at night.

He chills in the chair
With his feet in the air
And howls with all his might.

He's long haired and scruffy
And likes to watch Buffy
But we love him all the same.

James Parker (11)
Colmers Farm School

ALL ABOUT ME

When I woke to go to school,
Had a kick about with my ball,
When I had my breakfast I got dressed,
My sister came in, she's always a pest.
I went downstairs to catch the bus,
My mom called me back in a fuss
I got the bus with my sister,
My shoes were rubbing, they came out in a blister
I met my teacher Miss Hey,
She was a good teacher in a way.
Teachers help you when you're low,
I ask people where I have to go.

Anthony Poole (12)
Colmers Farm School

HOT DAYS

The hot days have come
The ice-cube's melting.

The children having water fights
With the freezing water.

The trousers go away
Out come the shorts.

And here comes winter
All over again.

Jason Coley (11)
Colmers Farm School

SATURDAY

Saturday, Saturday, it is Saturday
I can stay in bed till hal- past eleven
Or get up at half past seven.

I can eat all the food in the street
Or dance to a funky beat.

I can play the computer all day long
Or listen to my favourite song.

I can watch TV all night
Without flying my kite.

In the morning I'll be yawning
Because my dad's snoring.

Ian Barrett (11)
Colmers Farm School

THE SIMPSONS

The Simpsons are funny
They have lots of money,
Bart is a pain,
And Homer's insane,
Maggie's a pest,
And Lisa's the best.

Jodie Killeen (11)
Colmers Farm School

I Wish It Was Saturday

'Oh Mom do I have to go to school today?'
'Yes now get ready before you miss your bus.'
'But'
'Now!'

I wish it was Saturday so I could fly my kite
And spread my wings
Oh I do wish it was Saturday.

'Goodbye Mom.'
Nearly Saturday only five days to go.

Chris Lawrence (11)
Colmers Farm School

The Sun

Sun, sun come to play it will be a wonderful day
If you come out to play we will have lots of fun!
If you like me so come, come, come and play and have lots of fun,
I'll bring my rat and my little bat so we can play
And have lots of fun,
So come, come, come and play with me today
It will make me so happy today
So come, come, come and play and have lots of fun today
If you do not come and play I will be so unhappy today
So please, please come and play and I will be so happy today!

Charlotte Baker (12)
Colmers Farm School

SUMMER, SPRING, WINTER, AUTUMN

It's ever such a sunny day
The temperature is ever so high
It comes to thirty-two today
And every morning the sun looks shy.

All the flowers are round as a ball
They all are ever so pretty
They are big and very tall
But not as tall as my kitty.

Autumn has finally come
It's when all the petals fall off
All the flowers have a nice name
But it's sad because I have a bad cough.

Spring has just made it here
It came ever so quick
But when spring comes I have to say see ya
To my best friend Nick.

Winter is here it's ever so cold
And the snow is clear
The grass looks cold, high and clear and bold
And I always get called dear.

I'm ever so sorry I've come to an end
I'm ever so sorry I won't be back here
Be careful of the flowers because they will be sent
Thank you for listening, see ya.

Aaron Ellis (12)
Colmers Farm School

NIGHT OWL

She swiftly manoeuvres in the night,
Quietly stalking her prey
Then without warning she swoops
Down beside the weak creature.

Her babies remain in the giant oak trees
Waiting for their feast,
Then along comes their mother
With plenty to go around and around.

After a hard night's work,
She slowly drifts to sleep
Dreaming of what will come next.

Joanne Paintin (13)
Great Barr School

SEA

In the shark infested ocean,
A ship sails across the sea,
Waves clashing in a raging motion,
Will it safely reach the quay?
Bubbles rising to the top,
As divers search for a treasure chest,
Nothing in their path will make them stop,
This will be an exciting quest.

David Bonner (12)
Great Barr School

THE ROBBER

The robber's not left a trace,
He thinks it's a race,
He nicks everything he sees,
He has even nicked trees.

I don't know why,
But all I say is 'My oh, my',
You can hear him in the night,
He carries a torch, it's bright.

He wears a black hat,
And carries around a black and white cat,
He has a pink car,
And carries a metal bar.

Everyone thinks his name is James,
Because he always blames,
But I think he's silly,
That's why I call him Willy!

Willy The Robber.

Samantha Dangerfield (12)
Great Barr School

MY FRIENDS IN 7DG

Tracey Harvey is far from small,
She soon will be six foot tall
Laura O she loves to sing,
In fact she's good at everything.

Vicky with her Rockport shoes,
Thinks she's cool and flash,
With a Peter Storm and Sprayway coat,
Proves, she has loads of cash.

Laura J will be a vet,
Amy Poyner, a footballer yet,
Seth Pinnock a comedian is he,
Oliver Wilks is Noris to be.

Now a verse, it's all about me,
I enjoy any sport activity
Football, badminton and rugby too,
Academic subjects, I like a few.

Laura Denton (11)
Great Barr School

MOONLIT SPECTRE

In the moonlit night,
As owls fly by,
And the ancient clock strikes twelve,
You get a shiver down your spine,
From a ghostly scream.
As the last chime hits its clock
An indistinct figure walks past,
Disguised in its shroud.

Fearful carrying on I go
Then deathly silence, with unimportance to the world,
Dreadfully dark then without warning lightning strikes,
Wind howls, trees rustle, crows squawk.

And then I see it, waiting in the wings,
Waiting to get me
It jumps with its claws digging into me
A mask of horror before my eyes,
A gripping hand on my throat, squeezing,
And then blackness,
My soul has gone from the world.

Stephanie Somerfield (12)
Great Barr School

CHANGES

C amping out in my mom's belly!
H unting, hunting for food
A ll of my family were waiting for my appearance
N ans and uncles
G randads and aunties
E ven my big sister
S unday night I came out

I n my early years it was weird
N ow everything is and I understand.

M oney and more money was spent all on me
Y oung and sweet, that was me.

L ooking back in my life
I can see how I've changed
F orever looking back on what I did
E ven now I still remember.

Harry Walker (11)
Great Barr School

THE SINISTER GIRL

One cold harmful night
A young girl was very wrath
It was caused by annoyance
Because of the report she got in maths.

The girl is in a lot of trouble
By just walking down Blood Lane
She needs to turn right back around
Or else she will go insane.

Someone has put a Britney Spears album on
Her name was Leanne only to distract her
She followed the sound to 'Baby One More Time'
Then . . . somebody shot her.

There were police looking everywhere
However, they did not care
Therefore, she haunted everyone of them
In addition, she made them scared.

Keisha Lawrence (12)
Great Barr School

NIGHT OF FRIGHT

When I go to bed at night,
Everything turns to a fright,
My mom says it's all in my head,
And there's nothing under my bed,
My dad says go to sleep,
He doesn't want to hear a peep.

At night,
I turn on the light,
But everything disappeared,
But then reappears.

I do not want to turn off the light,
But I try with all my might,
As I do,
I hide under my sheets.

Then I go off to sleep!

ZZZZZZZZZZZZZZZ

Lisa Speak (11)
Great Barr School

THE ROARING GOAL

The ref blew the whistle
The players kicked off
The crowd started to roar,
Like a lion, at its dinner.

Like a game of tennis
The crowd watch the players run left and right,
But suddenly, one player turns to fight,
He slides along the floor
Watching the other fall.

The ref saw the foul
The fans all booed.
The ref pulled out his card times two
Watching the player walk off in a mood
Bye, bye player see you next game.

The player called out,
The free-kick was taken
The ball flew over the players' heads
Like a seagull over the sea.

The keeper was ready
The player kicked the ball,
The blast was so hard
The keeper started to fall,
What a diving header by Tony Hall.

Paul Eames (13)
Great Barr School

MY PETS ARE THE BEST

My pets are the best
I come home to find a furry ball
Lying on my bed and another one
Sleeping on the floor.
Guess who they could be?
My cats Jess and Sooty.

My pets are the best,
Rattle, rattle, goes a little ball along the floor.
She's white and hazel, she scuttles along the floor
Guess who she is?
She's my hamster Hazel.

My pets are the best
One and two I can see them now
Long, green and smooth
In their mini jungle they stick to
Twigs or your clothes
Guess who they are?
They're my stick insects Pinky and Perky.

My pets are the best.
I hear silence but two things move
There's something going up the tank
Guess who they are?
My fishes and snail, Smoky, Spot and Spec.

Amy Poyner (11)
Great Barr School

LEFT ALONE

The wide lonely tree,
Nothing in sight
Sobbing and uncared,
Shut out from the world
Nothing to watch
Waiting, feeling so unimportant.
It gazes up into the sky,
It begins to cry,
But people just walk by
Dropping water,
Not caring,
Just ignoring.
The tree only sees black,
The world seems so dim
Screaming out,
Waiting for someone to notice,
Thinking about the world,
Wanting to observe
The planet, the people,
So lost in thoughts.

Sharanjit Sahota (14)
Great Barr School

THE SUNSET

The sun is getting tired,
The sun now wants a rest,
The sun goes down slowly,
The sky is at its best.

It shimmers on top of the water,
Its rays so bright and fair,
Without a single problem,
Without a single care.

The colours are like bleeding paint,
Running into each other,
The sun is sinking down again,
It's going under cover.

Dionne Chisholm (12)
Great Barr School

THE RESTLESS COUNTRYSIDE

The sky got dimmer,
The air got angrier,
Clouds began to open up
They let out a loud cry
In the pitch black world.

Standing tall,
A tree with pointed fingers,
Stood by the side of the lake,
It reflected on the crystal-clear water.

Several horses ate off the chilly green grass,
That surrounded the field
They stood high and proud.

The fields were so far back,
They looked like they were shrinking.

Sun comes up,
Moon goes down
The world begins to activate again
Birds float over my head
Searching for their breakfast
Twenty-four hours of darkness have gone.

Shareen Lawrence (13)
Great Barr School

WAITING

The lonely lady sat waiting,
She was isolated in her own world,
Overlooking the surroundings
The time was ticking
The world was wondering,
And yet still no sigh
The clock on the mouldy wall
Sounds like drums to her
The door slammed it made her jump,
There was no one around but her
The cafe was closing,
She had to go,
So bitterly and painfully,
She abandoned the cafe
She was abandoned,
She felt friendless and betrayed,
With tears rolling down her face.

Dee Gallagher (13)
Great Barr School

THE SPIDERS

They skuttle across the ground,
Without making a sound,
Some are small,
Others are big,
Some are hairy,
I don't care they're very scary,
I don't care they're very scary.

I hate spiders,
I hate spiders,
Did I mention?
I hate spiders.

They scuttle across the ground,
Without making a sound,
Some are small,
Others are big,
Some are hairy,
I don't care they're very scary,
I don't care they're very scary.

Nateesha Toora (12)
Great Barr School

FIREWORKS

Illuminations in the sky, glittering as they fall,
Exploding light
Can you guess what they are?
In the dark, blue sky
They're fireworks.

Bright, delicate, sparks of light,
Purple, blue, red and green
Array of colours, all you can think of
Everywhere you look there's exploding light
Then . . . wow . . . a rocket zooms,

Up, up and away it goes up to the moon,
But before it gets there . . .
Bang!

Colours everywhere
Around and around
Colours you don't even know of
Gone . . . in the playground,
All that's left is cigarettes, crisp packets
Ashes
Nothingness.

Emily Wilkes (12)
Great Barr School

TWO-FACED

They're so two-faced,
I don't know why they do it,
They're so dishonest and haven't got guts,
I don't think they know what they're doing.

I can't stand these people
They can't confront anyone at all,
'Some things are better left unsaid to someone'
That's what they say,
But I think
Why say anything at all then?

Sometimes they don't even know the person,
They just go ahead and judge anyway
I know they don't like it when it's done to them,
Anyway all I know is that the outcome of
These people isn't so good.
They're so two-faced all I wonder is
Why?

Amandeep Sander (12)
Great Barr School

THE PERFECT STORM

The storm was brewing in the sky above the sea,
The lightning was striking,
The rumbling of the thunder,
And the crashing of the waves.

The storm was like a thousand bulls crashing together,
Clatter, clang, crash,
It was getting louder and louder and louder when . . .
Smash!
There was a tidal wave.

You could hear their screams for miles,
The storm carried on terrorising the city,
And the waves were as big as ever,
Smashing against each other and twisting up a tornado.

The tornado started travelling around the city,
All you could see was cars and houses flying around,
It was blood-curdling,
It sent a shiver up my spine!

Joanne Beddows (12)
Great Barr School

THE SILENT MOON

The vivid moon hid behind the clouds,
Popping in and out,
Shining on the ground below.
The moon glistened in the twilight.

Beaming, shining,
Glowing bright.
Flickering out of sight,
Covered by the clouds once again.

Emerging breezes,
Twinkling rays.
Clouds swirling round like whirlpools
The moon lonesome and still.

Fading rays,
Lighter skies
The moon was saying goodbye.

Julie Parry (13)
Great Barr School

THE SLAUGHTERED SOULS

As the troops approached in the landing craft,
There was a sudden sound of gunfire,
As they rushed out into the water,
Trying to take off heavy equipment before they
Could resurface.

On dry land they scrambled holding weapons,
And crouching behind metal structures,
It is like a nightmare come true,
Dead bodies scattered everywhere,
Grenades making sure they get the job done.

The German manning the machine-gun roared as
He mowed down troops with an evil smile.
More troops took position, trying to put the madness to an end,
But they knew they would not survive.

The carnage continued,
And it would not stop, the beach was not a good place to be
The sea has been turned a blood red,
And the number of casualties increases.

Suddenly an American bomber plane flew out of nowhere
And answered their prayers
As their messiah had just turned up,
The soldiers continued to fight.

'No one can guarantee success in war, but deserve it'
                          Winston Churchill.

David Ellson (12)
Great Barr School

STRESS

Stress, stress, stress that's all life's about
Pressure and stress I feel like I'm going
To bust if someone tells me something
Else they use me for a shoulder to cry on
Then she turns around and starts talking
About me with a friend who's supposed
To be my so-called friend
Sounds two-faced doesn't it?

I don't trust anybody, my friends
At least especially the ones who talk
About me behind my back.
I talk to them but I don't like them
The way I used to there's friction
Between me and her she knows
Something's wrong but too afraid to ask.

I don't worry myself about it most days
But to say they're supposed to be friends
Makes me feel sick and unbelievable.

Stress, stress, stress that's all life's about
Pressure and stress I feel like
I'm going to burst with anger
But what can I do, except confront
Them I already did they denied it
Then walked away and carried on
Talking about what just happened and
About me.
Stress, stress and more pressure.

Justina Maynard (12)
Great Barr School

WATER PARK

Beautiful blue paradise,
Angry waves destroying anything in its path,
A mix of soapy football sweltering sun and soothing showers,
Volleyball courts in unalloyed sands,
Pitch black shoots with splashing moves and turns before
Smashing into blue aqueous surroundings.
Vertical drops from absurd heights at cheetah-like speed,
Rock slides as tall as a mountain smashing against the sides,
Water riots in whirlpools the size of the ocean,
Amazing sites from the top of the towering rope and rubber structure.
Buoyant slides, glistening water and energetic people
Make water parks a place of everlasting fun.

Daniel Ullah (12)
Great Barr School

SPIDERS

Creatures with long scrawny legs
Like long thin twigs
Creepy like a tiger just
About to pounce
Spiders.

Creatures with fat bodies
Black like the night
Scuttling around day and night
Spiders.

Fast like a bullet coming out a gun
Big and horrible
Spiders.

Terri Gray (11)
Great Barr School

CHANGES

When I was born I was small,
Not able to talk, walk or barely see,
Changes, changes, changes,
When I was a child I used to play,
And be happy and full of joy,
Changes, changes, changes,
When I was a bit older I understood arguments,
Arguments with my brother, parents, friends,
Changes, changes, changes,
I started school and began to learn,
Learning by the minute.
Changes, changes, changes,
I got to my last year at primary school,
So much happening so much going on,
Changes, changes, changes,
Adjusting as I start seniors,
But getting tired,
Changes, changes, changes,
When I am older I will try hard at school work,
GCSEs come, work hard, try hard
Changes, changes, changes,
Leave school, get a job,
Work hard and earn a good living,
Changes, changes, changes,
I retire from work,
Bored, nothing to do.
Changes, changes, changes,
Suffering, become ill,
I die.
Changes, changes, and final changes.

Craig Wiggins (11)
Great Barr School

THE CLENCHING FISTS

The fists clenching,
The lips bursting.

The angry laughters,
The aggressive supporters.

A painful beating,
The eyes are bleeding.

A fearful fight, at the
Dead of night.

Boxers bruised like an apple
On the street, so rotten not good
Enough to eat.

It's a match of pain,
But the points need to gain.

The shiny red glove,
Like the sign of love.

Soon it will all be over as
Peaceful as a dove.

Jonathan Greene (13)
Great Barr School

THE RAGING TWISTER

As the twister crashes to the ground,
Trees go up, houses go down,
People are laughing people crying,
Only   because the wind is dying.

Then it comes back in command,
Conquering its village destroying the land.

Houses still fly while people cry,
While cars are crashing with a lashing.

The twister stops with a bang,
All you can see is the foggy smoke
And the greyness land.

John Gallagher (14)
Great Barr School

SPACE

S   paceship going into the starry sky,
P   eople, friends say goodbye
A   re aliens up there? Who knows?
C   ould it be, there she goes,
E   ars popping
S   paceship not stopping,
H   ere in space
I   t's a wonderful place,
P   lanets are gleaming and the sun is steaming.

S   paceman on Mars
P   acked together all the stars
A   liens, aliens there they go
C   ould it be, I don't know?
E   verything went quiet
M   an, it looked like a riot,
A   liens were everywhere
N   ext aliens run into their lair.

S   pace lit by stars and the sun,
P   retty Mars,
A   nd Earth and stars
C   ould anything be as nice as me
E   ither Earth or sea.

David Fox (12)
Great Barr School

ALIEN INVASION

Alien invasion on my planet,
Beep, beep, bleep, bleep.

'We're not going to harm you Earthling people,
Just to inspect your daily life.'

'We've come to enjoy this world's future,
To prance about and play
To find out all your mechanical and weird things,
Just to inspect your daily life.'

'We've come to try out and experiment with you,
Your cars, your trains and washing-up-machines,
The cogs turn round click, click, click,
We have come to inspect your daily life,
Your unusual civilisation.'

Stacey Collins (12)
Great Barr School

A CHILD'S DREAM

When I go to bed at seven,
I dream that I am up in Heaven,
Angels flying in the sky,
So good and perfect they've never told a lie.
Oh how I wish I was an angel,
With fluffy wings and a golden halo,
Living on a silky cloud,
Lovely peacefulness hardly a sound.
When I go to bed at seven
I dream that I am up in Heaven.

Gemma Hooley (11)
Great Barr School

GIRLS

Sugar and spice and all things nice,
So the poem says.
But that's not all there is to us,
We have many girlie ways.
We like to stand and 'make our face,'
And comb our hair for hours,
And scream and moan if we get caught,
In storm or snow or showers
Our make-up has to be just right,
Not one hair out of place,
A different hair style every day
A simply perfect face
When we go clubbing we must wear,
High heels and pretty dresses,
And perfume to turn every head
The boys we must impress.

Jenna Evans (12)
Great Barr School

THE SAVAGED GARDEN

The garden was quiet,
As the wind was whistling,
My dog started growling ready to bark,
The loud disturbing noise
All wild roses with sharp thorns,
The overgrown grass changing to a colour like brass,
The dark blue sky ready to die.

Ryan Parkes (13)
Great Barr School

DISASTER HOUSE

Running round the house got to go to school,
Can't get out of bed school will be a bore,
Trying to eat my breakfast, my brother's snoring loud,
I wish I was up in Heaven on a white fluffy cloud.

It's eight o'clock I'm still in my pyjamas on the chair,
I haven't brushed my teeth or even combed my hair,
My books aren't in my bag most of them are on the floor
I think I know my lessons I really am not sure.

The flower vase has got knocked over all over my RE book,
I hope there's a God up in Heaven cause I'm gonna need some luck,
I put it on the radiator hoping it will dry,
It's still soaking wet I gave out a great big sigh.

Running out the door at twenty-five past eight,
Praying to my God please don't make me late,
Half way down the path at home,
Then I start to hear the phone.

I finally get to school on time,
There's no one in the playground but I'm sure it's ten to nine,
Then a teacher comes out and starts to shout,
Go home it's teacher training day
I remembered that when I looked about.

Emma Forbes (11)
Great Barr School

MY MUM

My mum is like a flower, her love grows
Her love showers me with her golden glows
My mum gives out her praising light,
But when she shouts she gives me a fright.

My mum is generous and kind,
For sure she is the greatest mum you can find,
When I see my mum she brightens up my day
This message is to say I love my mum in every way.

Briana Bridgen (12)
Great Barr School

MY CLASS IN THE FUTURE

What will I be in the future?
To tell the truth, I don't have a clue,
Amy Poyner will be a football player,
But I don't know what I'll do!

I could be a spaceman, I could be a vet,
I could write love songs,
But that's far too wet,
Who knows what I'll do?

Seth will be a comedian,
So will Oliver too
Martin will work in a factory,
Melting bright green goo.

Laura Denton will be a dentist,
Don't have a clue what Katie will be,
But I'm afraid the question is
What will happen to me?

Adam will be in the convention of worriers,
Dominic will as well,
James will be a servant
Who stands at the gates of Hell.

Who cares about the future?
It's ages away!

Laura Jones (11)
Great Barr School

A BIRD

A fierce and dangerous animal,
Quiet and quick in flight,
Its life untroubled,
With its beak as a deadly weapon
In its armoury.

A barn owl,
Fast and peaceful,
Beautiful and wary,
It's free from the life we know.

A bird is also relaxed and patient,
With little worries and problems,
It is as calm as the night,
It is also independent,
Magnificent as it flies through the free-hearted air.

A robin,
Bright and colourful
Undisturbed and gentle,
Exploring the white snow for food.

Paul Sheldon (12)
Great Barr School

A QUIET NIGHT AT THE LAKE

Animals standing,
Staring at the lake,
The wind was silent,
Nothing was violent.
The lake lay proud,
Shadows lay on it,
Nothing could beat,
A quiet night at the lake.

The sky was dark,
The moon was full.
Nothing could be heard,
Not even a bird,
Fields in the distance,
The perfect view,
Nothing could beat,
A quiet night at the lake.

Sean Britton (14)
Great Barr School

THE PERILOUS SEA

The perilous sea is like a dangerous animal
Banging against its cage to get free
The dark lonely ocean clashes,
Upon startled cliffs
Foam from the waves scatters in all directions
The crashing waves show the oceans
Desperation for company
The ocean is lonely as it cries
For a companion
Seagulls screech whilst battling against the gale-force winds.

A boat is struggling in the ocean desperately
Trying to get home to safety
The deep sea prevents anything being seen
Underneath its dark cover
It would be impossible for any
Man or animal to cross.

Nicola Dorman (14)
Great Barr School

BROTHERS

Big and brutal
Small and screaming
Taking forever,
But still not gleaming,
Taking control
Never wants to lose
Brothers act the total fool
Want to win every game
Turned eighteen only want champagne
Messing around trying to be in
The place for them is in the bin
We know deep down they've got a heart,
So let's hope they use it before it falls apart.

Rachael Dean (11)
Great Barr School

THE CALM COUNTRY

The calm country was especially liked
By the cattle grazing,
That were shaving the tops off the grass
The creased leaves crunching underfoot.
The crackled branches seemed
Placed on the tree.
The clouds pushing over
And the soundless moon
Glows in the wind.

Natalie Hughes (13)
Great Barr School

THE NEW GIRL

The new girl Kerry Smith has just started a new school,
Everyone adores her and thinks she is so cool
All the teachers comment on how she is so neat,
Even the headmaster thinks she is so sweet
She is in everyone's good books and can do nothing wrong,
She hasn't even been with us for that very long,
She is so funny and has a great personality too,
There are times when you can play with her
When you have nothing to do
I helped Kerry when she didn't know her way around,
She even helped me when I fell to the ground
I don't know her that much, well what can I say,
So far, she's been a good friend in each and every way.

Lauren Jones (12)
Great Barr School

THE OUTRAGEOUS SEA

The outrageous sea is out of control,
The sea is thrashing into the rigid rocks,
The white frothy water trailing ahead,
Being pushed and tossed like a toy,
The lonely sea is crying out, it has no friends
The wind is blowing outrageously out of control,
The storm dies down
There was silence.

Ashley Wright (13)
Great Barr School

My Grandad

The house is busy everyone's running about
My nan's cooking
My brother's playing on the floor,
My mom's cleaning
My dad's painting the wall
No one's noticed the empty chair by the door
Where my grandad used to sit.
Why am I still remembering the day I dressed in black?
Everyone else has gotten over it and are getting on with their lives
So why can't I do that?

Zoe Wakefield (12)
Great Barr School

Spiders

As hairy as my hair and
As dirty as gardener's boots,
As creepy as ghosts at night.

As ugly as a filthy, ugly, powerful witch,
As small as an ant but with eight legs.

As big as rats but with eight legs
But with loads of eyes.

Spiders
I hate them.

Sian Crellin (11)
Great Barr School

THE THINGS I LIKE

I like to think of things I like
Like skating or riding my bike
I like to wear nice clothes and shoes
But one thing I hate is Winnie The Pooh
I like to wear the brand name Kickers
But I really hate to see frilly pink knickers,
Also I really like to eat and drink chocolate
I like to eat till I get fat
I enjoy watching horror films
Because up my back I get chills
My favourite film is April Fools
I thought that film was really cool
I like to read all different books
But to Harry Potter I get hooked
Another thing I really hate
Is the Teletubbies and when they come to play
Another thing is when I go out with my friends
There's Harry, Gary, Sam and Jen Jens
I like Eminem the rapping star
I really think he will go far
I like to watch things about cars
There's Driver with the carry stars
And there's Top Gear as well
I think that programme is really swell
Now I must go
So I won't say hello
And I will go.

Adam Fox (11)
Great Barr School

THE NEVER-ENDING STORM

The thunder was clashing the night sky
The thunder was roaring very blatant and descending,
The thunder rumbled and erupted the Earth
The thunder was ferocious.

The rain, fell and fell till the whole town was saturated
The rain, dropped as the clouds burst open
The rain drizzled in a shower
The rain, rapidly dropped with a force.

The lightning was striking ferocious
The lightning unloaded a massive bolt of electric
The lightning disturbed its electric current anywhere
The lightning lit the gloomy sky.

Craig Parker (12)
Great Barr School

HAUNTED HOUSE

Welcome to the haunted house
Be quiet as a mouse
There's lots of spooky things inside
If you're frightened you'll want to hide
There's frogs and newts and lots of toads too
If you see the ghost he's bound to say 'Boo!'
Be quiet as a mouse
Escape the haunted house!

Catherine O'Riordan (11)
Great Barr School

THE INTRUDER

The door slammed shut as I climbed the stairs,
The stairs that creak at every step.
I walked towards my bedroom door
The bedroom door that is starting to rust
I climbed into bed as the owls outside screeched,
I pulled the cover up round my head.
The windows rattled, the stairs creaked,
Noises outside nearly made me weep
I closed my eyes, I wanted to get to sleep,
To get to sleep, to worry no more.
But I heard a noise that awakened me,
The noise of someone climbing the stairs
My heart was beating boom, boom, boom,
I pulled the covers up to my eyes.
The hair on my neck, it had started to rise,
As I sat there in fear as the intruder climbed up,
Climbed up the stairs towards my room
I heard a final creaking, they'd reached the top
I sat and waited with baited breath,
Waited, waited, for them to enter my room
To get me, torture me, kill me!
Suddenly there was a creak, a slow, annoying creak
But it got quicker and quicker and quicker,
Until finally, I saw who my intruder was
A mass murderer, a crazy lunatic?

No, Just my mom back early from her holiday!

Laura O'Meara (11)
Great Barr School

A LITTLE ALIEN

I knew a little strange alien
Who was Albanian
Who had sandwiches for lunch,
And has a twin brother called Crunch.

His name is Fred
And spent all his time in bed
He lived in the country,
And talked to all and sundry
And had a job doing the laundry.

He was green and purple
And when he spoke he made a gurgle
He had big round eyes,
That looked like pies,
He had four arms
And he used them for charms.

Now I only see him once a year,
Because he goes back to Mars to look after his pet deer.

Laura Facer (11)
Great Barr School

STORM

The storm is fierce,
The storm is vile,
The storm is nasty,
The storm is over-powering.

The atmosphere is incredible,
The atmosphere is invisible,
The atmosphere is amazing,
The atmosphere is crazing.

The wind is mad,
The wind is bad,
The wind is horrible,
The wind is destructive.

The danger is fading,
The danger is dying,
The danger is moving,
The danger is going.

Aaron Pick (12)
Great Barr School

SPACE

S is for the sun which is boiling hot
P is for Pluto which is really cold
A is for the asteroids that form a belt
C is for the coldness when you step on Pluto's face
E is for the engine blast when they take off.

A is for astronaut
S is for Saturn with its rings
T is for turbulence when they enter the atmosphere
R is for the rings which go round and round Jupiter
O is for Orion's Belt which is beautiful at night
N is for Neil Armstrong first on the moon.
A are for aliens which are from a distant planet
U is for Uranus with its really large rings
T is for trouble when you run out of air.

James Wykes (11)
Great Barr School

SPIDERS

Spiders they are disgusting
And ugly like a monster
Trying to smile.

They are all creepy
And crawly and as
Fast as a jaguar.

They have such
Long legs they could
Almost wear gardener's boots.

Gemma Page (11)
Great Barr School

WORMS

Horrid as an ant,
Slithery as a slug,
Fat and bumpy like a caterpillar.

Wiggle as your toes,
They are very, very gross,
It's like a fat prawn.

Ugly and slimy,
Shimmering like fishes fins,
Small, quiet, leaving slithery gooey trails.

Sarah Handley (11)
Great Barr School

THE HARMLESS LAKE

The innocent lake,
Stands there confused,
The calm animals swarm across,
Licking the water
As they gather together,
They are pleased easily,
Warm, cosy, lovingly and passionate
As the moon awakens,
The lake ripples,
As if the lake was cold,
The tree begins to shake,
As the wind thumps through everything,
The trees lie there abandoned.

Leon Daley (13)
Great Barr School

HALLOWE'EN

Hallowe'en, Hallowe'en
Pumpkins, kids, trick or treat,
Hallowe'en, Hallowe'en,
Ghosts, goblins, witches, sweets
Hallowe'en, Hallowe'en,
Skeletons, blood, guts,
Hallowe'en, Hallowe'en
Death, death
Death
Hallowe'en!

Scott Hayes (11)
Great Barr School

THE MAN FROM BENGAL

There was once a man from Bengal,
Who got asked to a fancy dress ball,
He said I'll risk it, and go as a biscuit,
But a dog ate him up in the hall
His spirit flew over the town and heard a girl's scream
He felt like a hero, even though he was a weirdo
He found the girl being thrown into a car,
By a seventeen year old youth
Who looked like he came from Mars
Down he flew and beat up the young brute
Who was only an actor in costume
The director said cut
The girl muttered a tut
And explained she was late for a hair do
The director said he didn't care
As he sat down and did his hair
The man's spirit flew on, only to hear people's shouts and screams
He landed softly only to hear people scream more
He heard shouts of 'Ghost'
And said 'Spirits alive where?'
And started to panic like normal people would
He followed the screaming people into a little hut
Who locked the door behind them and didn't realise what was afoot
The spirit asked a boy who stood beside him if the ghost was gone
But only got answered with a scream and a yell
And then there was a terrible row
Chairs were thrown, people stumbled then the door slammed shut
He then realised it was he the chaos was about
He was the ghost, and he was going to have some fun.

Amanda Payne (11)
Great Barr School

THE GRIM REAPER

Walking towards you,
The dead black cloak,
Holding a blade
Coming towards you
Silently creeping towards you.

Into the dark, blood dripping off his blade,
The blade shimmering in the light,
A light flashes across the figure,
The figure cringes at the sight of the light,
Still advancing coming closer and closer.

Dragging his cloak along the ground,
Slowly, slowly he advances closer and closer
It stops and stares at you,
You stand as stiff as a rock,
Your legs clamped together.

Your eyes fixated on the figure,
Scared to death you try to run,
But your legs are transfixed
Your blood runs through your veins like ice,
Shivers running up and down your spine.

Lurking in the shadows it moves closer
You look and stare horrified by the figure,.
The figure catches the light you see its bony fingers
And its hood black as night,
Like a shroud of death.

Closer, closer it stops and stares again,
You still can't move,
Scared stiff you look at the road,
It splits in two with a burst of fire,
And the figure vanishes into the flames.

Michael Keatley (11)
Great Barr School

THE ILLNESS

The illness is like an outbreak of depression
Spreading through Northern Thailand
The disease sickens down inside of me
I examine an eighty-five year old man
He has suspected skin cancer,
He has an eating disorder,
Said he has had it before
His creaking bones gorge out of him
I sit and think
Why is being a doctor so pressurising?
Thought of people coming into me
So they can be cured
But
Here I am saying to myself
'Why am I in this job?'
The complaint, attack and cold and bitterness
That has come over me
I should be helping people
Curing diseases
Instead
Stuck here trying to understand my mind
It's filling up with sorrow, frustration and anger
Hostility and bad blood floods over me
What can I do?
Just do my job and - help.

Natalie Corden (12)
Great Barr School

THE INFERTILE DESERT

The impetuous thirsty desert
Sizzling with blisters;
The calm wasteland,
Wild and miserable.

The despairing outstretched land,
With no doorway
Wind streaming passed,
Taking particles of sand,
To a place of no return.

Russell Small (13)
Great Barr School

RATS

Black, dark eyes like a bottomless pit
They live in dumps and smelly parks
Oh rats they're nothing like cats!

They have big long horrible tails like a slivering snake.
They swim in lakes
Oh rats they're nothing like cats!

They have sharp teeth like silver saws
Rats, they're horrible creatures.
Oh rats they're nothing like cats!

Sarah Harper (11)
Great Barr School

SPIDERS, I DON'T LIKE 'EM

Hiding like a thieving spy
Always watching never cries.

It speeds past me like Denise Lewis
To fetch its pray for it to pass through it.

It crawls up curtains and up chairs
Like a baby who's learnt to climb upstairs.

Spiders who would like 'em.

Carly Woakes (11)
Great Barr School

MY HEARTBEAT

I can hear my heartbeat
Lying in my bed,
I can feel the blood rush
Pounding in my head,
Beating like a bass drum
In an empty room,
I can hear my heartbeat
Boomde - boomde - boom.

Richard Gregory (11)
Great Barr School

WAVES CRASH

She waits with anger
The tempest storm, screaming within her
Annoyed and furious with life
The storm she hates so much.

Waves crash, thunder roars
Her true love lost,
To the hands of the storm.

Her tears come down her cheek
Not knowing where to go,
The blustery wind in her face.

Waves crash, thunder roars
Is she willing to take her life
To be with the one she loves?

Lamara Brown (13)
Great Barr School

ENJOY COCA-COLA

C   oca-Cola - the best drink in the world
O   pen the bottle quick, I'm dying for a swig
C   rack, crack, crack goes the ice from the freezer
A   nd I pour it into my ice-filled glass.

C   old, freezing and refreshing
O   n and on it bubbles
L   urking in my stomach what an experience
A   lways Coca-Cola!

Laura Paterson (12)
Great Barr School

AIRCRAFT

I think any type of flight is amazing and breath-taking
I love the way the planes fly away and leaves a trail in its vortex
I always think the planes will eventually get to the heavens
And people will see their relations
And be pleasantly amazed
I would love to become a pilot one day
And fly over the sparkling sea
It is unbelievable how much freedom you have so you have no limits
I would love to walk across the runway with the stripes on my shoulder.

Thomas Barker (12)
Great Barr School

SPIDERS

Legs like twigs on a tree,
Sure they're not as big as me,
But I don't care.

They're as hairy as an old man's beard
But if there's fear you seek,
Then look no further!

Spiders
If you look closely and take a look
You'll find out how terrible they are.

Steven Magee (11)
Great Barr School

THE MAN WHO CAME FROM SPACE

There was a man who came from space
And everything he did was to do with that place
All he talked about was the planets
Mercury with it being so hot
Saturn with its long rings,
And Pluto being the smallest one of the lot
H   e said he has been to all of the planets
One by one, but nobody believes him at all
Then finally he goes off in his space shuttle
With a big cheer from the crowd
As he went back up into space

Simon Clinton (12)
Great Barr School

MYSTERY MOVEMENT

The salted sea swept the rugged surface,
Colliding with cold, dead rock,
Creating white foaming froth
Water swirling against odd abandoned rock,
The outrageous sea crashed out of control like a thunderstorm
Surely no one could survive in such atrocious current?
The movement of the sea is a mystery
What will it do next?

Nicola Yeomans (14)
Great Barr School

PATCHWORK STORM

The patchwork storm has just begun
Alarming the oceans by endless screaming and screeching;
The dark perilous sea clashed upon the cliff
Smashed harmful rocks, which out-casted across the ocean floor,
Sharp splashing waves dived into the mixture of colours.
Irregular colours chase each other.
The helpless alive sea rumbled boisterous;
Dangerously it smashed and crashed the weathered cliff apart.
The screeching, the howling,
Seagulls rising around the air current;
I feel unsafe as the storm rages around me.
The rocks thundering down from the cliffs
I'm unsure standing here.

Lucy Hudson (13)
Great Barr School

SPIDERS

Cobwebs like an old lady
Newly done webs shine like diamonds.

Spiders hiding in dark, deep damp
Shady corners.

Spiders hanging
Off walls or webs
Waiting to pounce on their prey.

Akilah Crandon (11)
Great Barr School

THE CHURNING WILD SEA

The murky sky glimmers
Over the black endless sea
The force of the waves crashing
Upon the rumbling, craggy rocks
As the sea swirls and churns
Round the rugged cliff.

This friendless sea holds many secrets
As the neglected cry of the wind goes on,
Abandoned
This alive and wild sea,
Unstoppable
As the storm sets in.

Leanne Wdowiak (13)
Great Barr School

SNAKES

His teeth are like daggers
As he bites his way through
A rat which is big and fat.

His green and yellow body slides across the floor
As the sun glistens on his hot smooth back
As he hunts for his food.

His eyes are like a devil's red angry eyes
As he looks round the forest with an
Evil look on his long thin face.

Stephanie Harbon (11)
Great Barr School

THE TIGER

The tiger's teeth are like arrow of daggers
When it hunts for its prey
And sticks its daggers into the prey.

The claws like fifty razorsharp pins
When it hunts for its prey
Is claws rip the prey apart.

The tail is like a whip
When it hunts for its prey
Its tail suffocates its prey.

Daniel Hall (11)
Great Barr School

SPIDER

Creepy-crawly as quiet as a hunter ready to get its prey
Silent, silent I am the hunter and the spider is the prey.

Every day is another day
Every place is another place
Every fright is another soul taken away from
        Me
Take my advice never run away from the prey
The spider.

Simone Barnett (11)
Great Barr School

THE INCREDIBLE JOURNEY

I'm shooting through like a shooting star
I'm in a big place, I've travelled far.
It feels very warm, am I being born?
Is this the start of my new heart?
As time goes by I'm getting larger
I've got a brain, I'm getting smarter.
I've got eyes, ears, fingers and toes,
All I need now is a nice small nose.

This place I'm in now has got a lot smaller
Could it be I'm getting a lot taller?
Lying and floating is all I can do
Is that a tunnel I must go through?
It looks so small . . . what a tight squeeze
What's this I feel? I feel a breeze.

Mummy, oh Mummy, what's this I see?
There are strange objects surrounding me.
The noise, the brightness I can't explain
Who am I? What am I? What is my name?
They use these things that they call toys
What joy they bring with all the noise.
The ones I like best are the lullabies
They help me to sleep as I close my eyes.

It's been a long day I'm sure you'll agree
What an experience, especially for me.
As for my mummy, she's earned her rest
For she has given life to only the best.

Patrick Hart (9)
Great Barr School

AT THE SEASIDE

At the seaside
Kids make sand castles
Mommies and daddies sunbathe
People go splashing in the sea.

Don't forget to put your
Sun-cream on or you will burn
Kids are eating ice-creams
Strawberry, vanilla, chocolate
Are very nice favours and
Sugary so they make your teeth rot.

Then we go on the pier
And lay on the machines
Mommy takes us round
While Dad goes to the cafe
To read the newspaper
And have a cup of tea.

Then we pack up the
Car and go home.

Katie Barker (11)
Great Barr School